C A P S T O N E

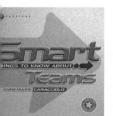

Stay Smart!

Smart things to know about... is a complete library of the world's smartest business ideas. **Smart** books put you on the inside track to the knowledge and skills that make the most successful people tick.

Each book brings you right up to speed on a crucial business issue. The subjects that business people tell us they most want to master are:

*Smart Things to Know about **Brands & Branding**,* JOHN MARIOTTI

*Smart Things to Know about **Business Finance**,* KEN LANGDON

*Smart Things to Know about **Change**,* DAVID FIRTH

*Smart Things to Know about **Customers**,* ROS JAY

*Smart Things to Know about **E-Commerce**,* MIKE CUNNINGHAM

*Smart Things to Know about **Knowledge Management**,*
TOM M. KOULOPOULOS & CARL FRAPPAOLO

*Smart Things to Know about **Strategy**,* RICHARD KOCH

*Smart Things to Know about **Teams**,* ANNEMARIE CARACCIOLO

You can stay **Smart** by e-mailing us at **capstone_publishing@msn.com**. Let us keep you up to date with new Smart books, Smart updates, a Smart newsletter and Smart seminars and conferences. Get in touch to discuss your needs.

C A P S T O N E

Smart

THINGS TO KNOW ABOUT

Teams

ANNEMARIE CARACCIOLO

First published 1999 by

Capstone US
Business Books Network
163 Central Avenue
Suite 2
Hopkins Professional Building
Dover
NH 03820
USA

Capstone Publishing Limited
Oxford Centre for Innovation
Mill Street
Oxford OX2 0JX
United Kingdom
http://www.capstone.co.uk

CIP catalogue records for this book are available from the British Library and the US Library of Congress

ISBN 1-84112-036-7

Typeset in 11/15 pt Sabon by
Sparks Computer Solutions Ltd, Oxford
http://www.sparks.co.uk
Printed and bound by
T.J. International Ltd, Padstow, Cornwall

This book is printed on acid-free paper

Substantial discounts on bulk quantities of Capstone books are available to corporations, professional associations and other organizations. If you are in the USA or Canada, phone the LPC Group for details on (1-800-626-4330) or fax (1-800-243-0138). Everywhere else, phone Capstone Publishing on (+44-1865-798623) or fax (+44-1865-240941).

Contents

What is Smart?

The *Smart* series is a new way of learning. *Smart* books will improve your understanding and performance in some of the critical areas you face today like *customers, strategy, change, e-commerce, brands, influencing skills, knowledge management, finance, teamworking, partnerships.*

Smart books summarize accumulated wisdom as well as providing original cutting-edge ideas and tools that will take you out of theory and into action.

The widely respected business guru Chris Argyris points out that even the most intelligent individuals can become ineffective in organizations. Why? Because we are so busy working that we fail to learn about ourselves. We stop reflecting on the changes around us. We get sucked into the patterns of behavior that have produced success for us in the past, not realizing that it may no longer be appropriate for us in the fast-approaching future.

There are three ways the *Smart* series helps prevent this happening to you:

- by increasing your self-awareness

- by developing your understanding, attitude and behavior

- by giving you the tools to challenge the status quo that exists in your organization.

Smart people need smart organizations. You could spend a third of your career hopping around in search of the Holy Grail, or you could begin to create your own smart organization around you today.

Finally a reminder that books don't change the world, people do. And although the *Smart* series offers you the brightest wisdom from the best practitioners and thinkers, these books throw the responsibility on you to *apply* what you're learning in your work.

Because the truly smart person knows that reading a book is the start of the process and not the end ...

As Eric Hoffer says, "In times of change, learners inherit the world, while the learned remain beautifully equipped to deal with a world that no longer exists."

David Firth
Smartmaster

Preface

You are well aware of the speed at which the world is moving, and keeping up with that alone is virtually impossible. In today's environment, where work is based on your knowledge, teamworking matters more, and making your team work well is what's important. Getting ahead in a world where knowledge and innovation are key success factors means collaboration and co-operation are the only ways to interact. It's no longer about climbing the corporate ladder by standing out as an individual; your team needs to be successful in order for you to be. And that's not just "rah rah" cheerleading, it's about how well you can handle other people. It can be great fun and at times a nightmare, but if you're smart, it will be an opportunity to learn about yourself as well as the people you work with.

But are teams a hoax – just another management fad? Or are they the only way to organize the workplace? Teams have become popular because businesses are operating with a leaner staff than ever before. It's a smart way to organize talent, and has obvious economic and competitive advantages, like a more effective use of resources. Let's face it, we're living in and through the era where companies have learned how to get the most out of what they have. Fewer people are doing more work, and there are fewer layers in organizations. Now add to that the speed at which information and communication is available, and ideas point us to the future.

Like virtually all other management jargon, the word teams suffers the same problem; it's inappropriate and overused. It seems that every time you have a bunch of people working together, they suddenly become a team. But that's not enough. You need more than just a label, you might as well be called a "bunch of asparagus" if you don't have all the basic elements and skills of teams and teamworking.

Most of the time you are hired, placed or promoted into a team. Rarely do you get to choose whom you want to work with. But, just because you are placed into a team, doesn't mean you can't make it work.

This book will talk a lot about what makes a team work, and define what teams are. But note now that there is a difference between teams and teamworking. Teamwork is a set of values and behaviors that helps teams to perform. These values also promote your performance as well as the whole organization. An organization with teams not promoting a positive set of values will suffer because all three are undoubtedly linked to each other; the individual, team and organization.

Teams, however, are not a set of values, they are the medium for teamworking behavior, and for getting things done. So when you hear people talking about the whole organization being a team, what they are encouraging is teamworking values.

In order for teams to work well, everyone who is involved with a team needs to understand how they function, and what's important.

Teams and teamworking involve not merely the intellect – understanding goals, tasks and approaches, but the emotions as well – understanding people, relationships and how people interact.

This book hopes to give you some ideas of what can happen, what it's going to be like, and what's the best thing for you to do while working in a team. Of course no book can give you the answers, life just ain't that simple, but just one idea might turn your team around.

Congratulations!
Today is your day.
You're off to Great Places!
You're off and away!

Dr Seuss, *Oh, the Places You'll Go*

Acknowledgments

Without the help and support of many people this challenge wouldn't have been a reality for me. Thanks to Sulwen Roberts for her patience and tolerance with the ins and outs and ups and downs. Nicky for always keeping the picture straight – in all respects. Annie and Liz for their life-long ability to be such damn good readers. Turn off the lights.

Mark and Richard for giving me the opportunity and being patient publishers. Rhona for great suggestions and firsthand experience.

Jane, Diane, and mom and dad for their support from afar and for always cheering me on. AXM for lots of encouragement and support. All the friends who kept me going with their sheer interest.

Romesh for his unending support, encouragement and partnership – kth.

This book is for Cara.

1

Teams 101

A lot of brains are superior to a few big brains.

Konosuke Matsushita

Each of us has our own experiences, expectations and ideas of what teams are all about. Because of those assumptions, it's smart to begin by drawing some distinctions between what teams are and how teamworking happens. There are also some basic, overarching assumptions that we take for granted about teams, like how important relationships are, as well as getting the job done. A lot of us don't realize that there are different types of teams with pros and cons associated with working in them. You also need some time to think about what you may be expecting from being in a team – and what you can gain from it, so check out the benefits available at the end of the chapter.

In a survey of more than 200 organizations across 16 countries and 6 continents, teamworking was listed as the third most important organizational competency today after customer service and communication.

If teams can add this kind of value to an organization, it is smart for anyone involved in a team to be skilled in understanding how teams operate.

Teams versus teamworking

The words *teams* and *teamworking* have been so overused that for many of us the concepts have been reduced to images of people having group hugs. But the basic idea behind a team, the reason to create a team, is to produce something that would not be so easily, efficiently or indeed possible to produce if you were working on your own. A team works together because the sum of contributions of the individuals is greater than if those individuals had worked alone. It's what *synergy* is all about (I know some more management jargon). In this light, teams make sense; put this way you can easily understand why so many exist in organizations. But smart teams get behind that basic idea and draw a distinction between teams and teamworking.

> **Smart things to say about teams**
>
> A successful team is when the sum of everyone's efforts is greater than each individual's efforts alone. It may sound a bit passé, but it still holds true.

Teams are the means to getting the job done; teamworking is the set of values and behaviors that help the team perform. So what is a team?

Let's look at how Jon Katzenbach and Douglas Smith in *The Wisdom of Teams* define teams:

- working towards common goals

- personal success of team members is dependent on others

- have an agreed and common approach

- knowledge and skills of team members are complementary

- a small number of people, usually less than twenty.

Katzenbach and Smith have been very influential in the study of teams. They advocate teamworking as common sense, but the implications are very subtle. They call this definition, the "team basics," and believe that if you focus on them along with problem solving, technical and interpersonal skills, then your team can deliver results. You may have seen this "definition" of teams before, but getting it together is tough. Don't get lulled into a false sense of security – just because you have all the basics" doesn't mean you have a good team. Teams are people, and we are by no means simple. Getting a handle on people is just as important as the goals and approaches.

We can define teamworking skills as:

- listening to others

- giving them the benefit of the doubt

- giving support when someone needs it

- valuing people's contributions and achievements.

KILLER QUESTIONS

- *Does everyone in our team understand the "basic" elements of a team?*
- *Can we distinguish the difference between teams and teamworking?*

Teamworking skills are about behaviors and they're not always easy to own up to or interpret. It's about communication and open-mindedness.

This is the really tough stuff. Unfortunately, you're a dead fish if your team doesn't have them.

One cannot exist without the other; to be in a team that doesn't understand the necessary behaviors of teamworking would be just as frustrating as having teamworking values, but no goals towards which to apply your behavior.

Why make such a fuss? You must see the difference if you are going to have a shot at being in a *smart* team.

To *team or not to team*

One of the basic, but all-too-often overlooked assumptions is whether you even need to be working as a team; it's one of the great management blunders of our times. The truth is there may be times when it's just not appropriate to be working as a team. For example, if you find you are working with others who have come together to share information or perspective, rather than to create a specific goal, you are working in a group. Groups don't expect their individual contribution to create added value to the whole. They may collaborate from time to time, helping one another by sharing best practice or information, but, unlike a team, they have no expectation that they will be working towards a specific goal.

Many times a team is authorized by "management" to exist without a clear understanding of whether the project really requires a team or not.

If you can answer yes to the killer questions below, then working in a team is the right configuration. But if the work can be divided among people

- Can the project be achieved only if individual contributions are combined?
- Do team members have complementary skills?
- Does the team have a clear and common goal?
- Do team members lead various aspects of the project?

KILLER QUESTIONS

Katzenbach is renowned for his work on teams and, as he is a director at McKinsey & Co., you would expect that his work isn't short on logic and reason. In his first book, co-authored with Douglas Smith, *The Wisdom of Teams*, he puts the issues of teamworking into clear and "business-focused" terms. He believes that, in order to be successful, everyone in a team must have the skills and behaviors that respect individuals and their contributions. He believes that if you focus on the goal, the skills and behaviors will come.

Katzenbach believes that team performance, is *the* objective function that matters. A real team is all about achieving higher-performance results, however defined. He believes that teams will outperform only if they pay disciplined attention to five basics:

- a performance purpose
- a clear set of performance goals that include collective (or joint) work products as well as individual work products
- a working approach that integrates the skills of all members
- a set of skills that is appropriate to the team's performance purpose
- a strongly held sense of mutual accountability that supersedes individual accountability.

Katzenbach recognizes that all too often teams lose their way. He believes that the way to get it back is to focus on goals and approaches, and that it's the basics that matter, but implementing them is a lot harder than it looks.

Katzenbach has also written *Teams at the Top* and edited *The Work of Teams*, which is a compilation of Harvard Business Review articles on team efforts.

SMART PEOPLE TO HAVE ON YOUR SIDE:

JON KATZENBACH

who do their parts and you can leave it to the leader to put things together, then trying to work as a team can prove to be confusing and frustrating.

Breaking things down like this may seem like splitting hairs, but these subtleties do make a difference. Teams were created by organizations to be more effective and efficient in getting the job done. But be careful how you use and hear the word *team*. Be sure you understand exactly what is meant by it. Is it just a word being used to describe people in a group, or is there some real commitment and value being added?

Relationships and tasks

Because teams are groups of people, you will always be managing not only the tasks but also the relationships. Throughout your work in a team, you will need to balance these two, paying enough attention to the task, but not forgetting that the relationships need to be maintained as well. So if your team gets stalled, you must determine whether the problem lies in the way that people are interacting, or the way you are approaching the job. People and relationships are by no means simple. In order to keep ahead as a smart person, you will need to develop your ability to understand how groups of people interact, and understand what's needed and when. Again this is just common sense – like most of this book – but common sense can get easily clouded in a team situation.

Smart things to say about teams

Teams don't become teams just because they are called that; it takes a lot more work and discipline.

So what does this mean? It means that you will need to be skilled not just technically or be a good problem-solver, but will need to understand people and how groups of people interact when they are working together. Impossible? People may come and go, but the basic processes and dynamics of how people interact in groups don't.

Types of teams

Teams come in many different forms. Since technology has changed the nature of working so much, we can no longer say your team members are always in the same building, country or department.

Some team types that you may come across include:

- functional teams

- cross-functional teams

- project teams

HP was founded in 1957 by Bill Hewlett and David Packard. They crafted the first set of corporate objectives that is still at the center of the company's management style, *the HP Way*. When Hewlett and Packard came together, they combined their product ideas and unique management style to found what is still a much sought-after place to work.

The company was formed on the belief that people want to do a good job, a creative job, and that, if given the proper tools and support, they will do so. Relationships are important at HP; the company depends upon co-operation and a commitment to teamwork. They know that it takes an attitude of trust and understanding on the part of managers towards their people and that employees must have faith in the motives and integrity of their peers, managers and the company itself.

But it's not all touchy-feely stuff, they expect the day-to-day-performance of each individual to add to the company's profit – and that profit is the responsibility of all.

SMART PEOPLE
TO HAVE ON
YOUR SIDE:

HEWLETT
PACKARD
(HP)

- self-directed work teams

- shift teams

- multi-cultural teams

- virtual or remote teams.

This list is by no means comprehensive, and you'll surely come across many other types. And while each type of team will have its own nuances, all of them will need to have the "team basics" and teamworking behaviors and values in place to be successful.

Let's take a look at the potential advantages and disadvantages for both you and your organization of these different types of teams.

Functional teams

- *What are they?*

  They bring together people from the same skill specialization to achieve a specific objective; like the book-production team or the journals-production team, both of which are a part of a publishing firm.

- *What are the costs?*

  Such a team is often set up without the appropriate people in it really needing to work as a team. Because you work together for a long time, the team may get stagnant. You may also find disagreement between functional teams, such as sales and operations.

- *What are the benefits?*

  The team works well because its members can get to know each other's styles and ways of working, and there is enough time to build relationships.

- *Smart moves*

  A functional team is a great place in which to develop long-term relationships, but there is a danger of its members becoming "type cast."

Cross-functional teams

- *What are they?*

  These teams comprise a group of people from various divisions or departments of the company, all of which have a different functional role, for example a team with someone from each of sales, marketing, production and finance, that are jointly responsible for product feasibility.

- *What are the costs?*

  At times it may not be clear who has authority and, if it's someone from one department, this may look very political. Also it can be more difficult to specify who the team leader is.

- *What are the benefits?*

  Because the team brings together departments or divisions that need to interact, decisions can be made more quickly and can break down cost barriers. It offers you a chance to see and understand the whole process of how your product and/or business works.

The whole is not the sum of its parts … but something much more, because the parts are interdependent. A tune is more than the notes that make it up; the bicycle remains a bicycle even after every one of its original pieces has been replaced. Contrarily, all the parts are not a bicycle, not until they are put together in one particular way. If every man looks at his own small task alone, ignoring its relationship to other tasks, the greatest productivity will not be attained.

Harold Leavitt, *Managerial Psychology*

- *Smart moves*

Ensure that all necessary functions are represented.

Project teams

- *What are they?*

They comprise a group of people convened to achieve a particular task, usually short-term, and then disbanded; for example a team to study work safety procedures.

- *What are the costs?*

Such teams can take your eye off your main responsibility or other projects on which you may be working. Often some of the individuals in the team have strong personalities which can easily clash.

- *What are the benefits?*

These teams can be incredibly effective because the focus is short-term and definable. There is often a great deal of enthusiasm for the project, because the team may be covering new ground.

- *Smart moves*

You may need to prioritize which project (if you're working on more than one) will be smartest for the business and your personal benefit.

Self-directed work teams

- *What are they?*

Such a team is responsible for a whole product or process; the planning, performing, implementing, co-ordinating and improvements.

- *What are the costs?*

These teams can be incredibly time-consuming, particularly at meetings. It may be difficult to understand and set boundaries around what decisions the team can and cannot make. As for the individual, you may get stuck with more responsibilities than in your "job description."

- *What are the benefits?*

Benefits include improvements in efficiency and customer service. Decision-making is pushed to the front lines; this means you can learn more about production and the overall business.

- *Smart moves*

Make sure that you aren't working independently and that problem solving and taking responsibility as a team is happening.

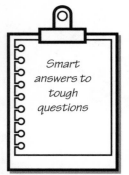

Q: Why do I have to worry about different types of teams; isn't that someone else's job?

A: Someone else in the organization may assign you to a team, but you'd better understand that that "type of team" will need more than just the basics elements to be successful.

Shift teams

- *What are they?*

  Shift teams are similar to functional teams, except that they operate a
  rota to cover 24 hours, e.g. a team of cardiac nurses.

- *What are the costs?*

  There may emerge a shift-A-over-shift-B mentality – "it's not our problem" – so compromising the end product.

- *What are the benefits?*

  The teams usually become highly cohesive, with their individuals communicating very well with each other.

- *Smart moves*

  Ensure that the methods and processes used for communicating are
  bomb-proof, and be diligent in sharing information from shift to shift.

Multi-cultural teams

- *What are they?*

  They comprise people from various countries/cultures and, as organizations continue to become global, such teams continue to grow.

- *What are the costs?*

  Such teams can fall apart if their members are not open-minded, patient, and tolerant of difference. Overall, interaction may take longer to develop.

- *What are the benefits?*

  You can gain a tremendous amount from the mix of individuals' skills and diversity. It helps if team members have mutual interests. Diverse teams have more potential than homogeneous ones.

- *Smart moves*

  Be especially tolerant to the diversity in the group, make sure you understand exactly what others mean. And be open-minded, turning diversity into an advantage by seeing the potential for new ideas.

Virtual teams

- *What are they?*

  Its members are located in various sites connected by email, teleconferencing and/or a net meeting.

- *What are the costs?*

  Effective and efficient communication can be a nightmare unless it's very well organized. If you need face-to-face contact and involvement, this one isn't for you.

- *What are the benefits?*

  Such teams are incredibly flexible because of the nature of their composition. Much information and perspective can be shared.

- *Smart moves*

  Make sure that there are structured communication processes.

This is just a brief understanding of what working in various teams may be like, but each experience you have is likely to be rich and challenging in its own way.

A survey of 51 companies in the *Fortune 100* rated the rank order of how companies benefit from teams:

1 Greater productivity
   Effective use of resources
   Better problem solving
2 Better quality products and services
3 Creativity and innovation
   Higher-quality decisions.

Expectations

When you think about work, you probably spend time worrying about your job, role and how you can contribute, but you may also have some expectations about being in a team. They may include how you would like to be treated, as well as ideas about influence in the group and whether or not you will have any.

You need to be clear about your own expectation as well as others. Also, while you may think, "I don't have any other expectations other than doing my job, doing it well, and getting along with everyone," don't ignore what may not be up-front and foremost in your mind.

Take a look at what your expectations are of:

- yourself

- the team

- the company.

Smart quotes

A team is not a bunch of people with job titles, but a congregation of individuals, each of who has a role which is understood by other members.

Meredith Belbin

When you look at yourself, figure out what you really want to get from this experience; is it just getting by, or do you want to make a mark? And what do others expect from you? Are you aware of how other people perceive you?

As for the team, what do you expect it to be like working with everyone? Are you going to be enjoying it? Is it working well together, or is this an environment in which cliques have developed? What expectations does the team have of each other – what do they value?

Aside from understanding what expectations you may have and others of you, do your expectations match those of the company? Is this an organization that pays lip service to teamworking, or do senior managers take it seriously and support teamworking?

Here are some smart steps to take to check out your assumptions:

- Understand your own expectations – once you understand and have thought about them, you can deal with everyone else.

- Estimate everyone's expectations and see how they match yours.

- Then get out there and check your observations against reality. This means talking and asking questions – cautiously. Check other people's commitment to find out what their expectations may be.

Once you have this information, you can put things into perspective. For example, if you find that other members of the team don't buy into the concept of being a team at all, you can spare the efforts to get everyone to work more closely together and "bond" as a team. Shift your expectations; you may be structured as a team and may all be working towards the same goal, but people will be working individually and without the support and drive of a cohesive team.

> **Smart things to say about teams**
>
> We all have expectations of ourselves and others, it's just a question of how close they are to reality.

Benefits for you

In order for the smart person to benefit from being in a team, it helps for the team to be successful, which is why you are spending time understanding how to make teams work. Also, being a part of a winning team gives you the potential to gain the following:

- *Networks*

  Where else do you have access to so many different people, some of whom will find your point of view interesting, or need your skills at a later date? The chances are that people move on from your team, whether internally or externally: being a team player will help you to develop those networks, and keep people interested in you.

- *Variety and challenge*

  This is a great time for different perspectives and experience. It's great exposure not only to other people, but their ideas and ways of working.

- *Personal pride*

  Not only do you gain pride and a sense of achievement in the quality of product or service, but also in the relationships you develop.

- *Involvement in decisions*

  You have a better shot at being influential in how things may work in the future as one of the team members.

- *Ability to innovate changes*

  Involvement in decisions implies the ability to influence and create changes.

- *Camaraderie*

  Not only does being a part of a team fulfill our basic motivational needs of belonging, but it can also be a lot of fun.

- *Personal growth and training*

  Team members need more skills to be successful, and this is a great time to hone your technical and interpersonal skills.

- *Testing your leadership skills*

  Your part of the project or specialized skills may enable you to assume a leadership role, even if only for a short period of time.

- *Rewards*

  If your reward system is tied to productivity, successful teams in general outstrip individuals – hoorah – more rewards.

Summary

This chapter has been an introduction to teams.

- It has defined and explained the difference between teams and teamworking;

- it has explained how important this distinction is;

- it has looked at different types of teams, and has examined the costs and benefits of, and smart moves to get ahead in, each of these types of teams;

- it has given you a chance to think about your own expectations of being in a team, and the expectations of other individuals and the organization as a whole;

- while on some level you may have already been aware of the potential benefits of being in a team, the chapter has spelled them out in greater detail.

This chapter is a smart starting point for developing and delving further into the world of teamworking.

KILLER QUESTIONS

Would you rather work as part of an out-standing group, or be a part of a group of outstanding individuals?

Max DePree, Leadership is an Art

2

What Makes a Team?

We must all hang together; or assuredly, we shall all hang separately.

Benjamin Franklin

This chapter will define in further detail what makes a team, and which elements are needed to be successful. It will also help you identify what you need to look for in a team, give you a clearer understanding of what motivates people and will emphasize the importance of the individual. It will look at the importance of culture to the success of both you and your team.

Let's go back to our definition of teams as described in Chapter 1 so that smart team-players have a clear understanding of what it's all about. The important point about teams and teamworking is that most of it is common sense and knowledge. So, as you read on, don't be surprised if you've heard some of this before. However, the smart team-player has learned to recognize whether a team is really making it work. And if not, where and why it's fallen down.

OK, here's the definition of teams from Chapter 1:

- working towards common goals

- personal success of team members is dependent on others

- have an agreed and common approach

- knowledge and skills of team members are complementary

- a small number of people, usually less than 20.

But what does that all really mean?

Common purpose and goals

It's pretty obvious that you must be clear about what you and your team want to achieve. But haven't we all been to a meeting where no-one seems to understand what's happening and why, nor can anyone figure out how to stop the vicious cycle from continuing? I call these "fuster clucks."

Take, for example, the senior management of a sports-car manufacturer, all of whom had been appointed in the previous 24 months, and who were determined to work together as a team. But they repeatedly had team meetings which seemed to roam, no-one stuck with the meeting agenda, and they all seemed to be pushing their

Smart quotes

All great teams – and all great organizations – are built around a shared dream or motivating purpose.

Warren Bennis

Peters and Waterman developed the concept *solution space*. A team is given a broad framework, by management, of the performance requirements of the company, and is then allowed to get on with things. But because it's a frame, it gives some room for modification when developing the goal.

own ideas forward. The problem was that, while they had the potential to be a "good" team, they didn't have a clear and common goal. They spent too much time being heads of their own department, where they were each highly successful. They thought all they needed was to bring their own department's agenda to the table and, because they represented the whole company, that would make them a team. They forgot the first smart lesson – have a clear and actionable common goal.

Teams get into trouble because, although they may have a goal, they find that all too often it isn't demanding enough, realistic, or not really a common purpose at all.

To avoid this trouble, it's useful to understand the distinction between *purpose* and *goals*. A common purpose is what sets the tone and aspirations for your team; a goal gives you something to do, and is usually a solution to the purpose. For example, Steve Job's and Steve Wozniak's purpose (aspiration) was to create a user-friendly personal computer that provided information technology for ordinary people. Therefore, their goal was to develop, market and prove that Apple Mac 1 and 2 were better than the competition. Their dream was to create the Mac, but the various aspects of the hard work – the development, creation and marketing – were the goals they set which brought their dream to life. This means that smart teams understand why they are together – what the purpose of the team is – what aspiration they are setting their sights on and how they are going to get there.

Demands usually come from outside the team, but they will give you the opportunity to shape your purpose. For example, the head of marketing wants to increase market share by 20%; that leaves your team in the position of coming up with a way to make it happen. "Management" have given you their aspirations – your team must now figure out what you are going to do to get there.

A smart team talks about its aspirations and goals. And that means spending a lot of time at the beginning of your project talking about how things are going to take shape. You must resist the temptation to think you have things under control because "we all know what we're supposed to be doing. So we don't really need to talk about it."

KILLER QUESTIONS

Can this team distinguish between its common purpose and goal?

Talking is going to keep you motivated and involved. Think about it, if you've spent time talking about what you want to achieve, how you are going to do it, and have truly collaborated, then there is a pretty good chance that your team will be motivated. There's something about being able to say, "that's my piece and I'm excited about doing it." It creates ownership and a chance to feel proud of your work. Do you think that "management" should be spending their time developing your team's goals? Sure, they should be involved, but imagine if you weren't? Fat chance you'll feel very motivated if you don't have a say in how you'll achieve someone else's aspirations.

But don't expect that you will always be clear about what is and should be happening, especially when you are in mid-project. That means you really need to keep talking and looking at what's happened, what needs to happen, and whether you need to move the goal posts or not.

As well as helping motivation, talking about your aspirations and goals will help develop an identity for your team. If you can identify what has to be done because you can see how you and each individual on the team is going to help make it happen, it gives you something you can hang your hat on. It's an added bonus that will come from the hard work you're doing.

The smart person won't expect talking through these issues to come easily; it may seem impracticable and silly to a lot of people. But if your team is struggling, and you know that it lacks direction, then keep pushing to have discussions about what your goals and purpose are.

Your goals need to be linked to the overall objectives of the organization. In order for that to happen, there must be communication between the team and management (or whoever is responsible for the organization's objectives). I know this sounds obvious, but you can imagine that some teams, especially self-directed teams, can lose sight of the big picture. This is not to say that your team may not be able to develop a product or idea that will open up new markets for the company (look at Dilbert, which certainly changed how publishers look at business books). You don't want to spend a lot of money and time pursuing a goal that in the end doesn't match the objectives of the organization. The smart lesson is to keep communication open between the team and management.

Smart answers to tough questions

Q: How can we take the time to talk about our goals and purpose if we are constantly under pressure to produce?

A: Without setting aside time to establish what you're after, your team will undoubtedly find itself wasting a lot of time back-tracking, trying to keep everyone working together and re-establishing what's happened and what should be happening.

Let's talk goals, specifically

Your team not only needs to have agreed upon goals, but those goals need to be specific and realistic, like a call-centre team whose goal was to answer every call by the third ring. The only way to know what you are going for is to be *very* specific. That means your goals have to be measurable. Let's face it, without the nitty gritty details, you don't have a very good chance of achieving your goal. For example, the infamous New Year's resolution: "I'm going to start going to the gym more often" sounds great and virtuous especially after the season's festivities. Yet, unless you specify how many times a week, or which days you're planning to go, you have no idea whether or not you really are "going to the gym more often."

Specific goals give you something to shoot for – a target. But not all targets are goals. For example, the sales and marketing team at an electrical utility was looking to increase market share by 25%, that was their overall goal. They began by going after the Northwest, developing a strategy and learning about customers in that specific area. Their target was the Northwest. Targets help you get to your goal.

Having specific and realistic goals may sound awfully boring, but without the details you'll find you're chasing your tail. Don't think you shouldn't be challenged; you are more likely to make a commitment when you are. Some drama, urgency and a little fear can be a great combination to give you a boost of drive.

Knowing what you are specifically trying to achieve helps keep everyone on track. If your goal is ambiguous or non-existent, then you are bound to have those meetings and discussion that never accomplish anything nor seem to end. Not that this is the only answer to communication problems, but it will keep the discussion focussed on the issues at hand.

Smart teams see each other for what each member can contribute towards getting there, not for what title or bonus you may have or can get. And teams with a specific goal to pursue do just that. There tends to be less mud-slinging in a team that sees its individual members for who they are and what they have to offer.

It's unavoidable, but internal politics and personality conflict are a part of working with people. If conflict occurs over personality, that's politics; but work-based conflict can be constructive. Conflict can bring to light new ways of doing things or help you see things from a different perspective – make sure it's just that. It's very important that counter arguments are based on real work issues, and not a difference of opinion or personality conflict. Play the devil's advocate, provided as you're introducing new ideas or ways of thinking.

Your team must keep both the overall purpose, and the specific goals alive and ticking. They are, for the most part, interdependent. The purpose keeps the long-term alive and the goals the short-term. But which comes first? Surely you must need an overall purpose before you can set a goal. Usually a team with a specific goal will find it develops into an overall purpose, for example, reducing production costs by 25%, which may lead to the decision to develop a bigger market-share. This is where those interim discussions become important and at times invaluable. Teams have meetings all the time, but how many of those meetings are productive? Do you have discussions about whether the goal is still appropriate? What are the long-term impacts for the whole business – for the team?

Establishing these fundamentals can be very time-consuming, and takes effort in good communication; but most great things happen very slowly,

> Carville and Stephanopoulos created an atmosphere with such a strong purpose – getting the Republicans out of office – that the goal – getting Clinton into office became a passion for their staff. They fired-up staff with "campaign" slogans, like *"it's the economy, stupid"* and *"change vs. more of the same thing."* These slogans which hung on a sign in the War Room were used to bring a focus (specific goal) for each and every thing that Clinton spoke about, and what he intended to change.

like baby steps, which can be totally annoying because most of us don't have much patience. But small steps forward will help to build commitment within the team.

Success is dependent on others

The personal success of team members is dependent on others. For the team and the individuals to be successful, you must be held accountable to each other. The culture of individualism we live in doesn't do much to reinforce this. So the whole thing sounds pretty scary. But imagine a baseball team trying to win a World Series without the players being responsible to each other. Conversations like "well, I know I missed that ball, but what can I do?" wouldn't go down too well in the dugout. Have you noticed how professional sports players are always so apologetic when

Smart quotes

> Individualism in our culture is deeply ingrained and, in a large sense, over-encouraged. Trusting one's fate, as one does in a group, to the performance of others can set off some mighty powerful personal alarms.
>
> Dave Blum (Reporter, American Society of Training and Development), January 1998

they screw up? Why? Because they know that they are held accountable to each other, they know the team is relying on them.

Letting your fate be determined by others is a concept that hasn't permeated our working culture. So the first thing to recognize is that doing this will not feel comfortable. It will be difficult to let go at first and believe that you do need each other, and that you can trust a bunch of people. The way to make this process easier is be sure your team has set down the foundation by putting in the hours towards establishing goals and approaches. Doing this is not only a good way to get the job done, but a great way to start relationship-building.

Smart people deliver and are held accountable for their end of the bargain. When someone delivers, don't you usually feel pretty good about that person? It means they are reliable and are willing to stand behind the work they've done. If you and your team are working together in this way, being dependent on each other doesn't need to be so scary. If you invest time into something, you begin to feel commitment towards it. So if a team invests time and real work into a project, then the more committed it will be, which means that team members can begin to trust and rely on each other. But remember these are behaviors that don't just develop overnight. They take time and work. Because you probably don't have a lot of time on your hands, it means that you'll need to put more emphasis on being reliable. That's why it's so important to deliver and be held accountable.

As your team works together, trust and commitment will develop, provided energy and action are being used towards doing some real work together. But often you'll find team members that feel half-hearted about the work the team is doing. The first question to ask is whether your team knows where it's going. Have you set goals?

Smart quotes

Everyone in attendance has responsibility for making sure the group is functioning properly.

Thomas Kayser, Mining Group Gold

If you have, then those goals can be used as a benchmark for team members. Because these are guidelines of the work that needs to be done, if you can't handle them or come to a compromise, then you don't belong on the team. Without commitment and participation you are letting everyone else down. Sometimes people stay in teams because they think that they have to be there, not because they are committed. Involvement in a team, means responsibility and accountability.

This isn't team blackmail either, you shouldn't be expected to be responsible and accountable for work that is above your skill level nor should you be "dumped" on.

Be clear about your approach

Having a clear, common and agreed approach means co-operating and pooling resources. It means understanding who's doing what, what the time-frames are and how you're going to stick to them. It also means deciding what your guidelines are going to be in terms of cost and administration. And how are changes and decisions going to be made? You also need to be aware, from the start, what the constraints are. Teams need boundaries, within the team and from outside. You need to know how far the team can go and what is expected of you, as well as knowing what is acceptable behavior within the team. Without these, you are heading for a fuster cluck. This isn't stuff someone else should be worrying about, if you're on the team you need to know or be a part of making decisions about these issues.

A common approach means agreeing on the specifics of work and how each individual's set of skills, talents, personalities, prejudices and job titles will fit in alongside what you need to accomplish. This means making sure that work isn't dumped on just a couple of people, just because they seem most appropriate.

It's going to take time to determine who's most appropriate in which roles. Different roles within the team will emerge as you start to work together, for example, the individual who wants to take the lead with regard to getting the job done, or the person who is good at inspiring and motivating the team. Don't think you don't have a good team unless you know from the start exactly who is going to fall into which role. Individual needs and abilities will depend on the situation, so don't fall into the trap of thinking that after the first meeting you must know who's doing absolutely everything.

KILLER QUESTIONS

Are we really working as a team, if the only time we get together is to have meetings updating each other on progress?

Do think about, discuss and adjust your approach relative to getting the job done. As your team works together, you'll come across problems and obstacles. Talking about how to approach them is the smart way to overcome them. It's easy to assume that "you'll cope with things as they come

SMART VOICES

When the Con-Way Transportation Services Information Systems department started to form in 1995, we wanted to create a mechanism that would help us when it came time for evaluations. We wanted something more positive than "appraisals" and "performance reviews," so we decided to develop a system that allows teams to evaluate themselves. We began by thinking about team performance and determined that the first and most important thing teams needed was a definition of excellent performance. So we developed a document called the *Team Agreement*. It sets out the definition of team performance, how teams do things and is know as our common law.

Fast Company, September 1998

up," which you will, but it'll be so much easier and smarter if you also have a mechanism in place to help you.

By now you probably feel, *ugghh!* all this book has done so far is spend time talking about how we are going to get things done – how impersonal. So how do we deal with the social aspects of teamwork? It always seem that the social side of working together seems to sort itself out, the people interested in going out just get on with it. Don't discount how important socializing as a whole group really is and how you need to acknowledge that from the start.

Smart teams don't just worry about whose going to get which piece of work, they also discuss and agree on what kind of behavior is going to be

A finance manager for a large international beverage company located in England was working in a project-team developing strategy to gain market share in Europe. It was a high-profile project, and they were under a lot of pressure to make it work. For some reason he found that his team was becoming less efficient. During a number of meetings, things would start to go off course, and some people weren't participating any more, even though he knew they had valuable contributions to make. It seemed like half the group was interested in taking things seriously, while the other half was somewhere else. He decided to get to the bottom of it and talked to one of the team members who seemed to have lost interest. He learned that a number of people were frustrated because the team didn't seem to take any breaks together. The only context they knew each other in was work. He and a few others were finding the pressure quite tough and they needed a break, but didn't want to go out on their own and create a "clique." This frustration could have been avoided if from the start of the project they established an understanding that they would need and want to take breaks together.

acceptable. For example, whether or not you can turn up the music, or go to a bar and finish a conversation there.

Knowledge and skills are complementary

We all have a mix of skills that we can call upon, some are technical, others are decision-making, and yet others are inter-personal. When a team starts out, it needs to know that it will have enough skills to work out what has to be done. This is especially true when you are talking about technical skills. You wouldn't want a programmer to run a financial audit. Make sure your team has the right technical, problem-solving and decision-making skills in place. And if they don't already exist, then get them through development within the existing team or by using outside help.

But we're also talking complementary skills. While the people with the necessary skills and knowledge need to be included, it doesn't need to be

Team work is inherently paradoxical, in that it comprises … contradictory elements, each of which is true. Team work requires differentiation among members and integration of members into a single working unit. The differences of knowledge, skill, experience, and perspective among team members are definitional. Without them, the … task cannot be accomplished, yet that task also demands that those different talents of insights be combined or integrated such that the members act as one. This seeming contradiction is nevertheless valid: The paradox of team work is that a balancing must occur between differentiation and integration.

Anne Donnellon, *Team Talk*

exclusive of anyone else. For example, the best people to develop a new product aren't necessarily just the people in R&D. Getting the right people together in a team can make or break it. Often teams are assembled not on the basis of how well individual skills may complement each other, but on how well people seem to get along, or what their titles may be.

It would be nice to think that all the knowledge and skills that you'll need in the future already exist within your team. The chances are that you don't have that perfect mix, and it's unlikely that you'll know in advance every single skill that will be needed in the future. The key is to be able to see where you have gaps.

OK, so do we bring people into the team to fill those gaps? That would be nice, but whose budget is that going to come out of and is it really necessary? Instead of being seen as a weakness, gaps create opportunities – the chance for you to learn and develop. It can be safely said that most of us have the potential to learn, it's just a question of whether you are open to learning or not. And while we're on the subject of development, there is the issue of interpersonal skills. Having interpersonal skills seems to be something you have or you don't. You either get along with people or you don't – right? True, some people seem to have the natural ability to do so, but for most of us it takes a little more work. Getting along with other people and understanding your impact on them, isn't easy – but if you have a brain, and you're willing to see other people's points of view, that means letting go of your own opinions and biases, then you have the potential to learn, even interpersonal skills.

The smart lesson is knowing that you won't need to have all the necessary skills within the team right from the beginning but you must be sure they are either developed within or brought into the team. And it helps if you have people who are open-minded to developing the skills necessary to make it work.

When Walt Disney created his studio of animators, he recruited 300 commercial artists, architects and potential artists from across the country. He provided training and other tools they needed, he didn't believe he could just hire them in and that their skills would already exist and complement each other. Disney wanted artists, so he sent them to night classes at Chouinard Art Institute of Los Angeles and started an art school within the studio itself. He had the ability to mold this team for things that they hadn't even anticipated.

Does size really count?

Well in this situation unfortunately it does. According to Katzenbach and Smith, teams that exceed 20 people are more difficult to manage, I think that 16 and greater can be tough to manage. It's just not possible to handle all those ideas, opinions and personalities and get anything done. It may be that you are working successfully on a project with such numbers, but remember:

- Large groups break down easily: there's too much information to take in.

- Everyone needs to be heard: your team needs a system in place that assures everyone is heard.

So if you are working in a group that is large, expect subgroups to form. This doesn't mean that teams bigger than 20 don't exist or aren't successful. They do exist, but they'll find it hard to be successful. Larger teams will have lots of communication issues to work through and again it's unlikely you'll find a team of, say, 35 that isn't breaking into smaller groups and then pooling back together.

OK, so we've talked through what Katzenbach and Smith call the *team basics*, which are crucial to team success, but about team dynamics? How do you recognize what's happening? Let's start by looking at the stages of development.

Stages of development

Teams go through stages of development. You can't plop a bunch of people together and expect them to evolve into a well-oiled machine after a few meetings. Because it's difficult to merge together the needs of people and the organization, it will sometimes feel and look a bit chaotic. So here are the stages of development in a team that will help you figure out what's happening.

- *Forming*
  The team is just getting together, orienting themselves, setting goals, clarifying expectations. It's an important stage for teams, because it gives you the opportunity to set out what your goals and approaches may be. It can feel a bit like a "honeymoon" period, where conflict is low but people are exploring what kinds of behavior are allowed.

- *Storming*
  Frustration and disagreement break out. Chaos and confusion may ensue, with the team being confused and stressed by the demands of the task and the conflict within the team. This is when roles are being decided, which leads to a great deal of discussion and argument. It's im-

portant that some of the conflicting issues come out into the open for the team to be successful, otherwise they may come up later on, holding things back.

- *Norming*
  Conflict and issues begin to be resolved and norms of behavior and leadership emerge. Diversity is accepted and a bond starts to form within the group. It's at this point that the team can establish what the team norms (rules of behavior) are, like what time the music comes on, what kinds of jokes are allowed, or who's going to do the research. It's time to set those boundaries.

- *Performing*
  The team is working well together towards common goals, productivity and team development. Things have clicked into place. The team starts to come up with solutions, gets on with the job to be done, and starts to enjoy working together.

During each stage you may also find yourself thinking:

- *Forming* – Can we do it?

- *Storming* – We can't do it because …

- *Norming* – We can do it if…

- *Performing* – We are doing it.

If you've been in a team before, you'll probably recognize some of these stages, and the storming stage may be the most memorable.

This model reinforces the idea that teams need to put time and work into establishing ways of working together. The storming stage seems to be the one most difficult to accept. And many times you will find teams look at this model and say, "oh, we are definitely in the performing stage," just because they are still all getting along with each other. What's really happening is that they still haven't moved out of forming. Don't be fooled, *you must go through each stage in the right order to be successful.* But how long will that take? It depends of course, on a number of things, like how long do you have to work together? A project team that has a working life of six months will have to develop quickly, while a functional team that is going to be together for years, will take longer, and may move backwards and forwards a couple of times if people come and go.

Another factor is how long your team stays stuck in any one stage. You can see the potential for getting stuck in the storming stage, but sometimes the forming can take a long time too. For example if your team won't state the obvious in the forming stage, i.e. what your common purpose and goals are, you can spend a lot of time spinning your wheels here. Or if you have a group whose members don't see how you are going to allocate roles and don't agree on what approach you will take, the storm will continue to brew.

It's pretty obvious that, in order to make it through the stages of development, team members must have created the teamworking values described in Chapter 1. You don't have a chance of per-

KILLER QUESTIONS

- Can we honestly say that we know what "stage of development" we are in?
- Have we really worked through the storming stage, and everyone believes that we can do it?

Smart things to say about teams

Don't forget that just because our team has moved forward from one stage of development to the next, doesn't mean we can't move back, perhaps because of changes in staff or leadership.

forming if you don't respect individual differences. Your team probably won't have these skills from the start; but smart teams have the potential to develop these skills. So what are they again? Teamworking skills are:

- listening to others

- giving them the benefit of the doubt

- giving support when someone needs it

- valuing people's contributions and achievements.

The smart team player knows that to entertain moving through the stages of development without developing these skills is impossible. But he or she also recognizes that they will take time to develop, not everyone walks through the door being open-minded and valuing their colleagues.

Individuals have needs

While Max DePree is right that the needs of the team are met when we meet the needs of the individual, this idea tends to be the most often and most easily overlooked element of teamworking. What with the targets and goals set within the time-frame that your team has to get the work done, who has time to deal with everyone's needs? So what tends to happen is that each one of us finds a way to take care of ourselves. Whether it's a sick day because you need a break, or a late night out with friends, no one can perform under pressure for a long period of time without some kind of reprieve. While those short-term reprieves may do you some good, what is the potential effect on your work? It won't do anyone any good if you've had a late night out and can barely keep your eyes open. Working in an environment where taking care of number-one is the only way to survive can be a cold and lonely place. Now don't get me wrong, I'm not advocating group hugs, what I am advocating is something in between.

OK, if the answer to the question, "what makes a team?", is "individual people," what does that mean for you? It means that understanding what people need and how they interact when working in a team is basic knowledge for the smart team-member. Remember that relationship-building, as well as task-achievement, is what makes a successful team. Let's be clear about relationship-building, it doesn't just mean how well you can get along with other people in the team, or how well you can get them to "like" you. It means understanding some of their basic needs and motivations.

> *Smart quotes*
>
> When we do not take other people as objects for our use, but see them a fellow human beings with whom we can learn and change, we open new possibilities for being ourselves more fully.
>
> Peter Senge, *The Fifth Discipline Fieldbook*

If we want to think about human needs and motivations, Abraham Maslow's hierarchy of needs is a good place to start. Motivation theories work on the assumption that, given the chance and the right stimuli, people work well and positively. Maslow believed that if our needs are tackled in order, as you get closer to satisfying one, the priority of the next one becomes higher. And once a need has been satisfied, it is no longer a stimulus. Maslow's hierarchy of needs is as follows (start from the bottom and work your way up):

- *Self-actualization*
  realizing individual potential; winning; achieving

- *Esteem needs*
  being well regarded by other people; appreciation

- *Social needs*
  interaction with other people; having friends

- *Safety needs*
  a sense of security; absence of fear

- *Physiological needs*
  warmth; shelter; food; sex

Maslow's hierarchy is a place to start, it takes into account the fact that people going to work don't just need money and rewards, but also respect and interaction. What it doesn't take into account is the fact that most of us want more and more money and are continuously upgrading our standard of living.

Let's face it, everyone wants some ***recognition*** for what they have done. No matter how you slice it, whether it's a research scientist who works alone in an ivory tower, or a member of your company's newest product team, we all want to be recognized and appreciated for what we have contributed. And many people want to be remembered for doing something great. How high we set our sights will vary and will, of course, depend on perspective. I mean how many of us expect to achieve the heights of recognition that Bill Gates has (OK, so you'll take the money and forget the fame). What this means in terms of teams is that you may have competing egos to deal with. More than one individual may be competing to make the same kind of contribution to the group. Smart teams give everyone the chance to make their mark in their own unique individual way.

Mayo realised the importance of self-esteem and group consensus. The *Hawthorne Studies* (1927–1932) proved to be groundbreaking work. Theory at the time believed that workers were motivated solely by self-interest. But Mayo found that workers had a strong need to co-operate and communicate with fellow workers. That productivity improved not because of changes in their physical environment, but changes in their social environment (remember, he was studying factory workers in the late 1920s). He concluded that:

- Work is a group activity.
- The need for recognition, security and a sense of belonging is more important in determining a worker's morale and productivity than the physical conditions under which he works.
- Workplaces are social environments, and within them people are motivated by much more than economic self-interest.

Mayo discovered a fundamental concept that seems obvious today, namely that people are motivated by more than just self-interest. Most of the "management gurus" of our generation stress the importance of the human side to work, a view surely originating in the Human Relations School.

Each and every one of us has our own set of skills and perspective that makes us not only unique, but able to contribute different bits and pieces to the overall picture. For example, some people are very good at coming up with ideas – give them a problem and they will throw more options and ideas at you than you may have thought imaginable. But put that person in a situation where they never have a chance to create new ideas, and you will have one frustrated team member. This means *respecting differences*. You'll more naturally "like" your team-mates if they are similar to you, but it's unlikely you'll have that luxury. So being open-minded and able to accept that people are more skilled in some areas than others and have different perspectives from yours, will be a great help.

Being *included* influences people and how they interact with each other. Whether it's a question of being asked to a meeting or to join a project team, people have a great need to be a part of something and to feel accepted. How do you think all those goofy clubs that exist in our society get away with it? Or why we get little groups that form around cult movies or TV shows, for example, *Twin Peaks*. If you were a fan and found someone in your office who also watched it, then you had this sense of belonging to something. Lots of people had *Twin Peaks* parties, eating cherry pie, donuts and drinking damn good coffee. But that need for inclusion can be so great that sometimes it can get you into trouble, for example behaving in a silly way (I have already given you an example of that) or, more importantly, you may find that you are unable to disagree, because of the fear of alienation (see the Abilene Paradox, Chapter 5).

Smart people realize that each individual has different needs, which vary at different times. For example, someone who is driven by the need to belong may not be interested in being made the next project leader, but more interested in being just a part of the team.

Culture

The culture within your team will undoubtedly be influenced by the organization's culture. Because we operate in a world of individualism, teamworking is a tough nut to crack for some. So while your team may have what it takes, some company cultures may only "pay lip service" to it.

How do you know whether you're in that situation or not?

- Look around you. Are there teams at all levels of the organization that you can say really work together as a team?

- Do teams have support systems, for example, are there opportunities for training and development for teams, not just for individuals?

- Look at reward systems. Do they reward the individual, the team or a combination? (See Chapter 6.)

Next you need to ask yourself whether you are really going to be happy in a culture of teamworking. Is this something you really want to do? Will you be able to attend collaborative meetings without grinding your teeth?

Apparently 95% of all firings happen because someone doesn't fit in with the culture, so these are important questions to ask yourself.

Cultures that are conducive to teamwork believe in learning. Teams need plenty of training and development, because it takes more skills to be productive and successful in a team environment than it does in a traditionally managed one. An organization that creates a culture where individuals

Smart answers to tough questions

Q: We are in a team, but how can we function effectively in a corporate culture that's not supportive to teamworking?
A: If you can develop the essential elements of a successful team (e.g. goals, approaches and teamworking values), then you may struggle, but have a very good shot at being successful. Then, when the organization recognizes your success, it won't have any choice but to support your team.

Senge developed the concept of the "Learning Organization." In his book, *The Fifth Discipline, The Art and Practice of The Learning Organization*, his message is simple: the learning organization values and believes that competitive advantage is derived from continued learning, both individual and collective. He has defined learning as "continually expanding our capacity to create the results we truly desire."

One of the core disciplines of the Learning Organization is Team Learning. He believes that the team's accomplishments can set the tone and establish a standard for learning together for the larger organization.

Team learning has three critical dimensions:

- *the necessity of insight into complex issues:* to tap the potential for many minds collectively to be more intelligent than a single one, because all too often the opposite happens
- *the need for innovative, co-ordinated action:* developing an internal relationship, where each member remains conscious of other members, and can be counted on to act in ways that complement each other's actions
- *the influence of team members on other teams:* a learning team continually fosters other learning teams through influencing the practices and skills of team-learning more broadly.

In 1994 Senge and colleagues published *The Fifth Discipline Fieldbook*, bringing much of his theory into practical terms. This book became a great catalyst for change in many organizations but, like most management thinking, it has evolved. In 1999 Senge and his colleagues from the *Fieldbook*, published *The Dance of Change: the Challenge to Sustaining Momentum in Learning Organizations*. It presents what they've learned about learning. It outlines the potential obstacles associated with becoming a learning organization, and proposes ways of turning these obstacles into sources of improvement.

Because companies are living organisms rather than machines, he believes that treating companies like machines inhibits change. We need to cultivate change, not drive it, which in turn means cultivating people and relationships.

Both books are available online at www.fieldbook.com.

SMART PEOPLE
TO HAVE ON
YOUR SIDE:

PETER SENGE

have the opportunity to learn, not only about themselves, but about other people and the work they are doing, is a pretty great place to work. But being in that environment doesn't always mean that you are going to learn: you have to want to learn and be able to take things in. It's partly about being a sponge and being open-minded as well as being able to filter and digest what's happening around you. But first you have to want to be that sponge.

This chapter has grounded you in what it takes to be a team. It has discussed in detail the "team basics" and has started to look at team dynamics by discussing the stages of development. We haven't forgotten the importance of recognizing individuals' needs, so we've taken some time to consider how important recognition and being included may be. Culture affects everyone, so we've given you the chance to stop and think about whether your culture supports teams and teamworking.

With the foundation now laid, it's time to start looking at some of the issues that come up when people start to interact.

3
Communication

Good communication is as stimulating as black coffee, and just as hard to sleep after.

Anne Morrow Lindbergh

Communication is inevitable. No matter what we do, we do it. Imagine an organization that couldn't get their message out through marketing or sales – they'd be dead in the water. But an organization can't just rely on advertising and sales, they must be good at communicating inside and out, to their customer as well as internally with their staff.

Because communication is such an important part of team working, this chapter begins by defining what communication is. Not that I think you are an idiot when it comes to understanding the basic things in life, but I do believe that it's important to begin by describing it in simple matters. Because we rely so heavily on communication, it's easy to forget that you can miss a lot in every day simple exchanges. And because I believe that *communication is the essential element that underpins success in your team*, I didn't want to make any assumptions.

If communication is that important, it means you'd better be capable and aware of what makes quality and effective communication. This does not discount what the last two chapters have had to say about teamwork, but communication is the foundation that you must build all your other work on. You won't have a shot unless your team is able to communicate well with each other. I'm focusing on communication issues within your team and the elements that will help you to communicate better. This chapter will also discuss the media we now use, and how things can go haywire using them, as well as some of the barriers to communication.

Basic elements

We communicate to share information with other people. Whether it's ideas, thoughts or feelings, to a big or small audience, transferring something that's in your head and making it heard (and understood) by others is what it's all about.

Smart quotes

The most important thing in communication is to hear what isn't being said.

Peter Drucker

When you start to analyze it, there are two elements of communicating, the content (what you say) and the process (how you say it). Most of us spend our time sifting through information, trying to figure out which piece of information to worry about right now. And *how* it is said sometimes dictates whether you deal with that information now or later.

Smart people balance the content and the process appropriately:

- *content* (the what) – thoughts and feelings

- *process* (the how) – verbal or non-verbal.

Content is what we say: for example, a colleague returns from a conference and reports what it was about. Included in that may be facts about what he's heard and seen and/or his thoughts and feelings.

The *process* we use to communicate, includes both verbal and non-verbal signals. The verbal includes not only the words being said, but the tone, inflection and emphasis that is put on words. Back to our example, that colleague who has just come back from the conference may change the way he *processes* what he's going to tell you, it will depend on what outcome he may want. For example, the tone, inflection and emphasis he may use would be different if he was seeking a budget allocation for a new product he saw.

Another example of how content and process work is cooking. I may have exactly the same oil, garlic, onion and fish (the content), but how I cook it (process it) will make it either an Italian dish or a French one.

Non-verbal signals relate to the feeling of what is being communicated. This includes body language. And body language plays a very big part in understanding what someone is saying. For example, it is believed that only 7% of our communication is represented by the actual words we use, and the remaining 93% by our non-verbal signals (see Albert Mehrabian). So, quite apart from being polite, you get a great deal of information from someone just by looking at them; like seeing the expression on their face or what kind of gestures they may be making.

Smart quotes

You can't judge people by what they think or say, only by what they do.

Major Kira, *Deep Space Nine*

Professor Emeritus of Psychology at UCLA Mehrabian is best known for his pioneering work in the field of non-verbal communication. His study in 1967 resulted in the *7-38-55 formula*. Mehrabian says that 7% of the meaning of a message is communicated through explicit verbal channels. That means that 93% comes from non-verbal communication. Of this, 38% is communicated by tone, the other 55% comes from visual cues, like gesture, posture and facial expression. So watch out: people are going to "listen" to your non-verbal cues.

It is confusing when your non-verbal signals don't match your verbal signals. For example, someone who says they're not angry, and then storms out of the room, slamming the door behind them. This is when differentiating between the words and the emotions becomes a smart skill to have.

Listen up

In order for people to communicate verbally or non-verbally, someone must be sending out a message and someone else receiving it. This happens according to the following process:

- receiving

- understanding

- responding.

Taken together, these are often termed "active listening." Nicola Phillips author of *Reality Hacking* describes active listening in three stages: obtaining information, evaluating information, and formulating a response.

- *Stage I: obtaining*

  The recipient understands exactly what the situation is. To do this, he or she must ask questions and listen carefully to the responses.

- *Stage II: evaluating*

  Breaking down the information into manageable concerns. To ensure that the information has been properly understood, the person needs to feed back what has been heard; check their understanding; and remove irrelevant material.

- *Stage III: formulating a response*

  Formulating an appropriate response to the information, which has been received, checked, and evaluated in the previous two stages.

Phillips believes that this is not a passive skill, but that you can use these "techniques" to help control the direction and flow of a conversation, and the amount and depth of information disclosed.

Smart quotes

... communication [is] the process of you receiving what I just said.

Eileen Shapiro, *Fad Surfing in the Boardroom*

But what is more likely to happen when someone starts talking to you? Steve Morris, Graham Willcocks and Eddy Knasel in *How to Lead a Winning Team*, explain that most people tune out once they hear something they recognize. For example, your colleague comes in to tell you about the fantastic skiing they had over the weekend. You skied there last season, and you start to remember the great times you had last year. What you end up missing is how so-and-so's boyfriend nearly killed himself when he slammed into a tree. Not only have you missed most of their story, but you have superimposed your own experience on to someone else's. As Morris, Willcocks and Knasel point out, "if you don't believe you do this, why is it that when you are introduced to somebody new at a party you have forgotten his or her name within the first four seconds? ... [It is] because you are not actively listening: you are more concerned about what to say, how you look or whether you will get to the buffet before it all disappears."

So what is active listening then? It's the skill of communicating through both verbal and non-verbal signals to the other person that they are being both heard and understood. It means turning off that little voice in your head for a minute or so, and concentrating on what's coming at you. It means not evaluating, judging or figuring out if what they are saying is logical or not. It means asking open-ended questions that are very specific which will open up the subject area.

But the balancing act is to not probe so far that the speaker gets defensive or insulted. For example, *why?* questions. It seems that when children go through the *why?* stage, most parents get frustrated and annoyed because they are being asked the question too many times. Add to that, *why?* can feel accusatory. How many times can you be asked "why is the sky blue?" before you start to feel really incompetent that "because it just is," isn't good enough and, worse yet, you don't really know why?

KILLER QUESTIONS

Is it just me, or does it seem that it's almost always easier to get people to talk than it is to get them to listen?

Active listening is a key part of communication and it would do most of us a lot of good if we all started listening more to each other. It's always easier to get people to talk, but getting people, especially a team of people together, to listen is quite another thing.

A team of seven men who worked together on an oilrig went on a team development course. One of their first exercises was to identify the shape and color of the two missing pieces taken out from a set of 30 unusually shaped pieces they were given. They weren't allowed to pass the shapes among each other, were blindfolded, and were only allowed to ask the question, "what color is this?" After the first minute or so of confused conversation, all was quiet, all seven men sat with their shapes in their hands, trying to work out what they were holding. Suddenly one of them started shouting, "calm down, calm down, we can do this if everyone just calms down!" Not only was everyone very quiet but they seemed quite calm as well. He was obviously having a tough time hearing that it was now quiet in the room.

Techniques for getting information

It's already been mentioned how you can use different "techniques" to increase your communication skills (active listening) and in doing this obtaining more information, and a better understanding of what someone is trying to say. But another technique, taken from Neurolinguistic Programming (NLP), is also useful.

NLP was developed in the late 1970s by Richard Bandler (a mathematician) and John Grinder (a professor of linguistics). They became interested in studying people who were excellent communicators and catalysts of change for others. They wanted to understand what created the difference between someone who is merely competent and someone who excels at the same skill. Their work helped to develop how we perceived the world and organize our thinking, skills, feelings, and behavior. NLP is defined as:

Smart quotes

For most of us, thinking that we have "tuned" into the other person, [we] are usually listening most intently to ourselves.

Warren Bennis

- *Neuro* – nervous system through which experience is received and processed through the five senses

- *Linguistic* – language and non-verbal communication systems through which neural representations are coded, ordered, and given meaning

- *Programming* – the ability to organize our communication and neurological systems to achieve specific desired goals and results.

They believe that you can code and reproduce successful results. The ability to do anything new or differently depends largely upon the ability to influence thinking patterns, to reprogram the mental processes and network of internal resources that we have.

Let's look at the Neurolinguistic Programming (NLP) model of communication. First an external event occurs; we then filter this by one of the following:

- deleting

- distorting

- generalizing.

And deletion, distortion, or generalization occurs because of our attitudes, values or memories. We then create an internal representation of the event; it leads us to a certain state (emotional feeling), which leads to some kind of behavior (response). Each of us also has a physiological reaction to that external event, but these tend to be more unconscious. These events do not happen in isolation of each other, they feed back to each other.

Smart answers to tough questions

I think the idea that we delete, distort or generalize information as it comes in, is key to understanding communication. When you realize that everyone has their own filters, it's easier to understand that we all hear things differently. And if those filters relate to our values, feelings and attitudes, you can also understand how over time as you get to know someone you begin to understand their filters.

One of Bandler and Robbin's techniques to obtain information is to learn how to ask questions by "chunking" down, up, or sideways.

- *Down* – gives you the specifics of something, for example, a bathroom. When you chunk down you get information like, it has a toilet, a sink, a bathtub. Or it's my bathroom with my sink, toothbrush, etc. "How?", "how exactly?" and "can you explain?" are downwards-chunking questions.

- *Up* – chunking that same bathroom up would give you answers like, "it's a room that is part of a house." Questions you would ask might include, "what is this an example of?", "why?", "what's the purpose?" These are bigger-meaning questions.

- *Sideways* – you're looking for comparative information, so you'd be asking questions like "what is an example of this?" or "give me another example of," "what else?", "where else?"

Understanding that you are able to get information from others through this process is a great tool, not only because it allows you to get more information but you can "chunk" in whatever direction you want to get different *kinds* of information.

This description does not give you a complete understanding of NLP. But this aspect of it offers a good technique to use for getting information, it's just a question of what kind of information you are after and what you plan to do with it.

Communication media – didn't you get my email?

Now let's look at some of the media for communicating with each other:

- *face to face* – meetings, formal, informal, in the same room or a videoconference

- *written matter* – memos, letters, and emails.

Face to face

We've already discussed what you can get from face-to-face interaction:

Smart
answers to
tough
questions

Q: Why bother checking that other people understand what your saying, it's so much faster and efficient to just say it?

A: That's true, but imagine you were trying to communicate something fairly complicated to team members, and they didn't have the opportunity to question you about the facts and any oversights. It leaves a lot of room for misinterpretation and misunderstanding. They don't necessarily doubt your knowledge or skills; they just want to be sure they get it.

body language, facial expressions, and the person's mood, all of which give you more information on which you can base assumptions and gain further understanding. It can, however, be easy to misunderstand someone's body language. This is particularly true if you are working in a multi-cultural team. For example, the difference between the Japanese and American's when they first greet someone. No body or eye contact for the Japanese, just a polite and modest bow. For American's hand to hand, smile to smile, eye to eye, anything less is considered not engaged or even unwelcoming. So, while body language will add value to your interaction most of the time, be sure that you understand the cultural norms with which you are dealing.

You can use more than one sense (sight as well as sound). In fact Abraham Lincoln was a big proponent of this; he thought if you used two senses you had less chance of misinterpretation.

Smart quotes

Communication takes imagination and patience.

Patrick Stewart as Jean Luc Picard, *Star Trek: The Next Generation*

One of his fellow law partners recalls his habits:

Mr. Lincoln's habits, methods of reading law, politics, poetry, etc., were to come into the office, pick up a book, newspaper, etc., and to sprawl himself out on the sofa, chair, etc., and read aloud much to my annoyance. I have asked him often why he did so, and his invariable reply was, "I catch the idea by two senses. But when I read aloud I hear what is read and I see it, and hence two senses get it and I remember it better, if I do not understand it better."

Donald Phillips, *Lincoln on Leadership*

So, according to Lincoln, two senses are better than one, maybe we should start reading all our emails aloud to remember them better ...

Smart answers to tough questions

Q: Why do I feel as if I can't get any work done? I seem to spend the whole day responding to the 50-odd email messages I receive every morning.

A: You need to use email more efficiently and learn to deal with what's there in the morning before 9:30, otherwise you'll end up spending the whole day responding rather than doing any proactive work.

The written word

Now the advantage of *writing* is, quite obviously, that it's there in black and white, and if it's a cover-your-butt type of organization, then you'll probably be spending lots of time putting things into writing. Unfortunately, so will everyone else. If you have that much information coming to you in the same medium, then it can start to lose value. It becomes more an issue of how to get through all your mail without spending your whole day doing it.

Another disadvantage is it's often difficult to express emotions and feelings (non-verbal signals get lost) and can be confusing to the receiving party.

Technology's changed it

Now look at how technology has affected these media; now you've more choice for interaction, for example:

- email

- video and conference calls

- voice mail.

Leavitt is a management psychologist, whose book *Managerial Psychology* is considered one of the best on the subject, in particular on the interactions and communication patterns of groups and the distortions that arise from links in the communication chain.

His more recent work with Jean Lipman-Blumen is about *hot groups*: "a lively, overachieving, dedicated group that is usually small, whose members are turned on to an exciting and challenging task." Although they tend to be temporary, they do great things fast. For example, Apple Computer in its "adolescent" years and AT&T gave Bell Labs the freedom to be a laboratory for hot groups.

Even though they believe that small, close-knit sets of motivated people are replacing the individual as the organization's "fundamental construction material," they also believe that hot groups don't survive in organizational management as we know it today. Most groups we live with now are overplanned from above. Hot groups aren't planned, not in the usual sense.

Situations that can help to develop a hot group:

- communication is open and access across organization boundaries is easy
- crisis or competition stimulates action
- truth is valued by the institution
- enthusiasm for a task leads to the spontaneous eruption of a group.

They also list a number of conditions that stimulate a hot group's growth:

- the presence of a task that is both intellectually and morally worthy
- route markers that signal progress
- a sense of community
- a hands-off attitude from the top, particularly in demands for immediate results.

Leavitt and Lipman-Blumen believe that when we try to "design and build" hot groups, they fail, and that, in order to develop, they need to be fertilized rather than constructed.

SMART PEOPLE
TO HAVE ON
YOUR SIDE:

HAROLD
LEAVITT

The great value that email has added to our world is that it is quick and easy, and this has made it an inherently more casual way of interacting. The danger is that it's too easy to be casual, and many folks have been upset and/or confused by casual emails.

It's easy to assume that the information in an email has:

• been received by the correct party –

• who has *read* and *understood* it.

For example, a large snack-food manufacturer found that it had to be careful with email addresses. Three junior staff had the same names (Tom Jackson, Anne Williams and Sue Parker) as three senior HR directors, and people wondered why there was no reply when confidential information appeared to be going down a black hole.

There are all kinds of assumptions you can start making when you don't get a reply from an email. Add to that how much it is abused, for example, the 250-page document that you really don't need to read, but someone thought you might find the 159th page interesting.

But, given that half of us switch off in meetings, email can be a good way to get your point across. I recommend that you send it before the meeting. You then avoid the danger of people totally switching off and saying "send me an email with the details."

Email is a great medium, but be careful that it doesn't get overused and abused. Communicating with each other is hard enough you don't need the technology to get in the way.

A marketing manager at a large software company consistently received copies of an email sent to her boss from a team peer in Europe. In the correspondence her peer expressed his concern about her role in the team, basically he didn't see the point of her job or her contribution. Luckily her boss was a good manager, and arranged a meeting between her and the peer, where they had a chance to talk through her responsibilities as well as his misunderstandings.

Video and conference calls

The idea behind developing video conferencing is to give you the face-to-face advantages without having to be in the same room. It's a "step up" from a telephone conference call, but both have similar frustrations. While they've made the world all that much smaller, if you ask anyone who has to use either, especially video on a regular basis, there is still a great deal of frustration.

According to Brigitte Jordan and Karen Ruhleder, because the resolution on video calls is still so bad, you can't look into the remote persons' eyes, and tell where they are looking, so you can't tell if they are paying attention. And if you are on a telephone conference call you don't even have bad resolution.

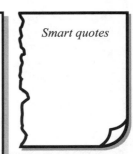

Human interaction is largely based on a turn-taking system. When "John" talks, "Susan" watches, says "Uh-huh," and nods so that John knows she gets what he's saying. Then it's her turn. If he looks confused or says "Huh?", that's a trouble flag. Susan knows immediately that there's a problem, and she can correct it on the spot ... Everybody thinks that video helps, but video makes it worse.

Brigitte Jordan (Xerox PARC) and Karen Ruhleder (University of Illinois)
CW Communications, July 1998

Video also creates a delay, at best a one-second transmission delay, which takes away cues and displaces feedback. So you'll find yourself talking at the same time as someone else, and it creates a lot of hesitancy while you wait for someone else to speak.

With telephone conferences you don't have the transmission delay, but you do have problems with cues and feedback. Often you'll miss the cue that they've finished because you can't see them, and everyone still starts talking over each other.

Because so much information can be flying around at any one time during a team meeting or video conference, you have to have very good listening skills, and you have to know your colleagues well to develop a good understanding in the team about how to communicate.

Be aware of the problems with video, voice and email, and use them only when they will help communication within the team, not hinder it.

Barriers to communication

The most obvious barriers to communication are language and cultural differences. But as I'm sure you are aware, barriers exist within the same language, same culture, and same organization. Barriers to communication can be as subtle as a noisy distraction from outside the room, to ideas you have in your head about yourself or team mates. Undoubtedly some kinds of barriers will exist in your team. Smart teams first recognize what those barriers may be, and then they try to get rid of them.

Here are some examples of communication barriers:

- *Status barriers* – fear of disapproval or a loss of face can be driving forces behind this barrier. For example, being afraid to admit you don't know what everyone is talking about, because you think you'll look stupid, so you go along with the conversation, nodding when you think it's relevant and laughing when everyone else does, but you're not really sure why you are.

- *Already listening* – you expect someone to give you the same message that they usually do. For example, Sam always talks about intranet links and how important they are ... blah blah blah. So you hear what you expect him to say, not what he really is saying.

- *Day-dreaming* – let's face it, that particular point being made right now isn't half as important or interesting as thinking about what you're going to do tonight.

- *Hostility or an emotional barrier* – something may trigger anger or annoyance, so you don't really hear what's being said because you're more concerned with how you feel about it.

- *Selective listening* – you hear only part of what is being said, and usually it's what you want to hear. So that bit about how your department's responsibility fits into the picture suddenly gets deleted, and all you hear is how everyone else has screwed up.

- *Cultural attitude* – the attitude that has developed in a team (or organization) about what types of communication are allowed, for example, a

As part of her role, Coley liaises daily with the US, Europe, and Asia Pacific. Strong advocate of regular face-to-face as well as virtual meetings with people to develop understanding and relationships. "Even video conferencing cannot replace the impact of face to face meetings where gestures and moods are easier to interpret. As well as the immediate feedback of group agreement or dissention."

team which only "allows" space for factual conversations, because feelings are "unprofessional."

- *Not enough is said* – a group's "atmosphere" may perhaps be too quiet, and someone may think that a particular piece of information is not relevant to everyone else. For example, one of the regional sales people didn't let the rest of sales team know about the change in attitude of some of their customers.

- *Too long* – the speech, conversation, diatribe that just went on and on: be aware of how long you are talking for. Most of us have short attention spans, so don't overlabor things. If you must deliver a long speech be prepared for people to lose track and interrupt you for clarification.

- *Rehearsing your response* – when you spend time worrying about how you are going to reply, instead of listening to what is actually being said.

- *Loaded questions* – setting someone up to respond in the way that you want/expect them to. For example, "don't you think we should share that ice cream, instead of you having to eat it all by yourself?"

The solution to many of these barriers is to put aside your own fears and preconceptions, by turning off your inner voice and concentrating on what

George and Emily just didn't get along. They worked side-by-side in US government-bond sales, and had two very different approaches to life. He had two Ivy League degrees: she had gone to a good university but had become good at what she did through work experience. She believed that what mattered was what you know, not how you got that knowledge. He believed that status and the old boy's network were at the heart of success. He believed that there were right and wrong ways of approaching things, she was more open to ideas. No matter where or how they tried to work together, it ended in dispute. During one of their "idea sharing" sessions with the rest of the sales team, Emily thought that a particular bond was a trading at a discount (good value). But, because George had such strong negative feelings about Emily, he was unable to hear what she was saying and to recognize a bargain. He heard only that it was coming from Emily. He couldn't bring himself to recommend the bonds to his client base and missed a great offer for them as well as the opportunity to rack up some decent commissions for him, and increase the numbers for the overall team.

is being said. If you find yourself responding emotionally to someone, you must focus on what they are saying, not how you feel about them.

How can your team avoid some of these barriers? First by accepting that they are bound to exist. Second by trying to identify where things are going wrong. But most importantly your team needs to encourage communication. Encouraging communication is smart.

People who are crystal-clear communicators know what impact they have on people around them, and are incredibly successful.

Solicitor at a London family-law firm

Smart things to say about teams

Sharing information … is the right thing to do. You never want to hide what you're doing or create suspicion about your motives.

Allan Cohen (Babson College), *Power Up: Transforming Organizations through Shared Leadership*

Common language

If you're in what Warren Bennis and Patricia Ward Biederman in their book *Organizing Genius: The Secrets of Creative Collaboration,* call a "Great Group," then communication will be non-verbal. Members understand the shared vision so well that they don't need language to communicate. And, they believe, very often these groups develop a language of their own, a kind of group speak.

What does it mean to have a common language? It's reaching a level of understanding where your team becomes more aligned, because, as Bennis and Biederman indicate, you understand the shared vision. For example, coal miners work more effectively because they understand their shared vision – to get the job done and to do it without anyone doing something that may risk their lives. They work under stressed circumstances and, in such a constricted environment, they must learn to communicate quickly and effectively, quality is just as important as speed. They each must de-

The most effective teams I've ever seen are the guys in the coal mines. Once you get down there all you can see is the whites of their teeth and eyes, but they can communicate more effectively than any team I've seen.

Mike Cambray, *Learning Partnerships*

velop a deep understanding that becomes second nature – they must align themselves to each other.

Unlike the coal miners, most of us don't work under physically threatening circumstances, but nonetheless in environments where speed, quality and mutual understanding are vital to success. And in order to achieve that, your team must create a common language.

Smart teams that are very clear about their vision and goals inherently have a common language. And they get there by talking through their understanding of what the vision and goal is.

Dialogue

One way to create a common language is to take time with your team to examine what is taken for granted. Peter Senge developed the idea that teams need to develop a way of learning to think together, a kind of reflective learning process. He calls this "dialogue." It is defined in *The Fifth Discipline Fieldbook* as:

… a sustained collective inquiry into everyday experience and what we take for granted. The goal of dialogue is to open new ground by establishing a "container" or "field" for inquiry: a setting where people can become more aware of the context around their experience, and of the processes of thought and feeling that created that experience.

Dialogue is not merely a set of techniques for improving organizations, enhancing communications, building consensus, or solving problems. It is based on the principle that conception and implementation are intimately linked, with a core of common meaning. During the dialogue process, people learn how to think together – not just in the sense of analyzing a shared problem or creating new pieces of shared knowledge, but in the sense of occupying a collective sensibility, in which the thoughts, emotions, and resulting actions belong not to one individual, but to all of them together.

At MIT (Massachusetts Institute of Technology) where Senge is based, a Dialogue Project has been established, which spends time "nurturing this process" for different organizations. So while we don't expect you try this at home, there are smart things to learn from it.

Dialogue proponents believe that the effectiveness of teams and organizations comes from how we as human beings perceive the world. We get stuck in our own distinctions and thoughts and, as the physicist David Bohm suggests, fragment thought. For example, marketing sees production as the problem, production sees distribution as the problem; that spe-

SMART PEOPLE
TO HAVE ON
YOUR SIDE:

ASDA
SUPERMARKET
GROUP

Besides valuing teamwork, ASDA gives employees the opportunities to talk. At the head office, staff attend a daily meeting where they are kept informed by their managers of what is happening that day within their sections. But it's also a platform where individuals can air their views or do a bit of complaining. The company believes that by stressing the importance of sharing it will reduce absenteeism and improve staff morale.

ASDA also has a program called the *Tell Archie* (Archie Norman is the Chairman). It encourages staff to propose ways that stores could be better run and customers better served. Staff whose ideas are implemented – and many are – receive star points which lead to cash bonuses or extra vacation.

Electrons cooled to very low temperatures act more like a coherent whole than as separate parts. They flow around obstacles without colliding with one another, creating no resistance and very high energy. At higher temperatures, however, they began to act like separate parts, scattering into a random movement and losing momentum.

William Isaacs on David Bohm in *The Fifth Discipline Fieldbook.*

cialists can not talk across specialities. We don't reason together, but defend our "part," and then seek to defeat others.

As Bohm describes electrons, it's easy to see the similarity of people to electrons. When everyone's temperature is high, we begin to act like separate parts. That's where "dialogue" comes into play. The underlying assumption of Senge's work is excellent, but putting it to work on a day-to-day basis, is not recommended without a skilled and experienced facilitator who clearly understands this kind of work. Getting into these deep issues can unearth a lot of feelings that shouldn't be aroused unless they can be dealt with professionally.

But every team has the potential to:

- suspend our views and observe the way that we have acted on assumptions

- question the total process of our thoughts and feelings

- listen to ourselves and ask the question, "where am I listening *from*?"

This chapter had a humble start, it began by defining in very simple terms what communication means. It developed the simple definition by looking at the importance of non-verbal signals and the skill needed to differentiate between the verbal and non-verbal. But the most important point about communication is not how you talk – but how you *listen*. And how we process that information will have a great impact on how we react to each other.

You've also had the chance to look at NLP as a technique for clarifying and getting more information. We looked at the impact technology has had on communication, and how you should use that technology, so that it helps rather than hinders your interaction. We've also looked at some potential barriers to communication for your team.

Last but not least, you've had the chance to see that creating a common language means that the team is more aligned, because it has reached a high level of understanding of its shared vision.

4

Team Leadership

There is nothing more difficult to take in hand, more perilous to conduct, or more uncertain in its success than to take the lead in the introduction of a new order of things.

Niccolo Machiavelli

To some people it may seem like heresy to say that teams need leaders – doesn't that run counter to the idea of co-operative working? It definitely should not. Leaders are important to teams because they can clarify goals, build the team's commitment and confidence, and create opportunities. A leader is also someone who may have to make some tough decisions, decisions that the team can't make on their own. And leaders can add expertise to a team – if they have it.

Teams are ultimately accountable to the organization, and it's nice to know that there's someone who can deal with the outside world – whether it's removing obstacles, or reporting progress upwards and outwards. So don't worry, having a "leader" doesn't strip teams down to an old-fashioned hierarchy: teams need leaders as well as members in order to be successful.

So why have so many of us had "bad" experiences with a lot of leaders? When organizations began to reconsider leadership in the 1980s, the military played a big role. The idea of the business world being a battlefield, with business leaders as generals inspiring the troops, was undoubtedly appealing. But the thinking and practice that developed out of that was command and control. It left the impression that leadership is anti-democratic and anti-team. Luckily, thinking and actual practice have changed. Smart leaders keep things democratic and team-like. They are also flexible and adaptable, able to recognize what needs are missing in the team, rather than just doing what feels comfortable for them.

Current thinking on leadership has moved beyond the idea that a leader needs to be charismatic and visionary. The focus now has moved on to being both people- and task-oriented. Smart leaders look beyond the individual leader to the team who, undoubtedly, will have a variety of leadership skills, thus making followers more powerful, able to voice their opinions and shape the way that an organization works. Smart leaders need to seek the support of followers more than ever. Just blowing the horn and barking off the commands won't help.

Don't get me wrong, there is some value in being charismatic, and that doesn't mean being superhuman. It means having the ability to enthuse, build morale, motivate and play a very large part in team effectiveness.

Leadership advice seems to exist everywhere, from business gurus to orchestral conductors. This chapter will focus on leadership *within teams*. Therefore, you need to understand both how teams work and what leadership means.

Defining leadership

It seems easier to define what leadership isn't rather than what it is, perhaps because there is neither a formula nor set of rules to follow. Because leadership is about leading *people*, rather than problems, it can seem ambiguous.

Leadership may be defined as:

... inducing followers to act for certain goals that represent the values and the motivations – the wants and needs, the aspirations and expectations – of both leaders and followers. And the genius of leadership lies in the manner in which leaders see and act on their own and their followers' values and motivations.

James MacGregor Burns, *Leadership*

Leadership is being able to point the way forward, having vision, as well as the ability to build teams and motivate people. And smart leaders are able to do that without compromising values and motivations.

Smart quotes

Leader: a person whose enormous flaws are exceeded only by the fit of his or her even more enormous abilities to the needs of the future.

Eileen Shapiro, *Fad Surfing in the Boardroom*

Smart things to say about teams

Leadership is the wise use of power. Power is the capacity to translate intention into reality and sustain it.

Warren Bennis

So if there are no rules to follow, and no formula to figure it out, what are you left with? Smart leaders are left
with their ability to adapt, learn and behave in ways that
foster the appropriate skills, attitudes and techniques that
each situation and team calls for. Awareness of what the
team is trying to achieve and achieving them is key, but so is
a leader's attitude, knowing that he/she doesn't have all the answers, and in fact that the people closest to the problem are
more likely to. That means you don't necessarily have to make
all the key decisions, nor do you have to provide all the answers.

Sounds great, but what happens in practice? Lots of leaders get
caught up in the ego and control factors and find it difficult to let
others do the work. Smart leaders know that a balance must be
maintained between doing the work yourself and letting others
get on with it.

Because leadership is seen as something one person does, it is generally
believed to be anti-team. But teams need leaders. Leaders cannot do the
work on their own, nor can teams be expected to make all the tough decisions themselves. Again, smart leaders strike a balance between providing
guidance and giving up control.

How to gain followers

Getting people to follow you is what all the leadership rhetoric is about.
Imagine being a leader and finding that no one is willing to follow you –
nightmare. The most important element to gain followers is that people
have confidence in you. But how do you gain that confidence? Some advocate that you need to sell yourself, articulate your ideas, and see things

Jon Katzenbach and Douglas Smith, authors of *The Wisdom of Teams*, believe there are seven necessary elements of good team leadership:

- Keep the purpose, goals and approach relevant and meaningful.
- Build commitment and confidence.
- Strengthen the mix and level of skills.
- Manage relationships with outsiders, including removing obstacles.
- Create opportunities for others.
- Do real work.
- *Never* blame or allow specific individuals to fail, and *never* excuse away shortfalls in team performance.

through. These are undoubtedly important elements of leadership. Delivering the goods does not merely get the job done; it builds confidence.

One of the best ways to get people to accept you as leader is by being one. But what does that mean, and how do I get there? Gillian Stamp, Director of Research at BIOSS (Brunel Institute of Organization and Social Studies) has developed what she calls the Tripod of Work – tasking, trusting and tending.

Tasking ensures that work adds value by defining the limits for judgement and agreeing criteria for review:

I'm a leader only if there are people who will follow me. A project doesn't move forward unless people buy into it. You cultivate followership by selling yourself, articulating your ideas, and developing a reputation for seeing things through.

Terri Kelly (W.L. Gore and Associates) *Fast Company*, November 1997

Bennis is one of the most widely known leadership gurus. He has written 26 books in his career to date, but *Leaders: the Strategies for Taking Charge*, co-written with Burt Nanus was his greatest success. Bennis studied 90 leaders from different professions and identified four vital competencies of the successful leader. They are:

- *management of attention* – the vision of the leaders commanded the attention and commitment of those who worked for and with them in attempting to achieve it.
- *management of meaning* – the leaders were skilled communicators, able to cut through complexity and frame issues in simple images and language. They were expert distillers of information.
- *management of trust* – trust was seen as the "emotional glue binding followers and leaders." For the leaders, trust was expressed through consistency of purpose and in their dealings with colleagues and others. Even though people sometimes disagreed with what they said or did, the leaders were admired for their consistency of purpose.
- *management of self* – the leaders were adept at identifying and fully utilizing their strengths, and accepting and seeking to develop areas of weakness.

Bennis believes that it is possible for people to learn how to become leaders, and that the key initial step is to learn to be themselves and to be true to their nature. At the time this had a dramatic impact on leadership thinking and brought reassurance to many that felt they weren't "born" charismatic leaders.

With Patricia Ward Biederman, Bennis wrote *Organizing Genius: the Secrets of Creative Collaboration* which was an update of his thinking. He was now interested in studying what Margaret Mead called "knowledge-based groups."

Bennis studied what he believes were some of the most noteworthy "Great Groups" of our time including: the Manhattan Project – the people who brought us the atomic bomb; Xerox's Palo Alto Research Center (PARC) and Apple Computer.

Bennis believes that at the heart of every Great Group is a shared dream. And alongside that is the redefinition of the roles and responsibilities of leaders. Despite their differences in style, leaders of Great Groups share four behavioral traits. Leaders of Great Groups:

- provide direction and meaning – they remind people of what's important and why their work makes a difference
- generate and sustain trust
- display a bias toward action, risk taking and curiosity
- are purveyors of hope – they find tangible and symbolic ways to demonstrate that the "group" can overcome the odds.

Bennis says that there are no simple recipes for developing these skills, that "group" leadership is far more an art than a science.

- sharing intention

- agreeing objectives

- agreeing a completion time.

Trusting ensures robust decision-making by:

- entrusting people with the purposes of the organization/team

I didn't have the opportunity to prove myself, and I didn't gain their trust. You can't lead if no one will follow.

Christopher Barnes, talking about a failed attempt to lead a team from Challenger Electrical Distribution, *Fast Company*, February–March 1998

SMART VOICES

• trusting them to use their judgement in doing the work
  they are accountable for

• evaluating and developing individual capabilities

• making sure that no-one is either "under" or over-
  whelmed by the challenges of their work.

Tending ensures that things keep working in the face of
time, change and uncertainty:

• the work assigned is still relevant – especially important in rapidly changing circumstances and when different cultures come together

• processes and systems are monitored to ensure that resources are being
  used appropriately according to current priorities

• a sense of purpose and relevance is communicated so that individuals
  have a context for their work, their initiatives and their judgement

• procedures are agreed beforehand for use in case of unresolved differences of view.

It's based on these three assumptions about how and why people make
organizations work. If you don't believe in these assumptions you'll have a
hard time working with the Tripod. The three assumptions are:

• Everyone needs to be able to exercise their own judgement in order to
  feel that they have completed their work well, and it makes the assumption that generally speaking everyone wants to do it well.

- Once tasks are assigned and people are trusted to complete them, then resources must be used effectively, and that the purpose is still relevant and significant changes in the environment are responded to.

- Everyone needs at all times to be aware of the objectives, how they fit into that purpose and how they will be contributing as their part is played. They need to feel they belong to something that is worth belonging to, and be kept aware of changing purposes. They also need to understand what is regarded as important overall, because they need that knowledge if you are to exercise your judgement appropriately.

> **Smart quotes**
>
> You can be appointed as a manager but you're not a leader until your appointment is ratified in the hearts and minds of those who work for you.
>
> John Adair (creator of action-centered leadership)

People can't operate in a vacuum, they need to know what the score is, why it's important, what the changes might be and why they, the individual is important. You can't expect team members to use their judgement unless they know what is relevant. So here's a smart tip – leaders need to be good communicators. In fact if you walk away with anything from this section it's that.

Leadership roles within teams

Generally speaking, leader means singular, the one that "oversees" the team. While leadership does exist outside a team, it also does within the team. Teams have two leadership roles that must be fulfilled. They are:

- *task leadership*

- *maintenance or relationship leadership*.

> **Smart quotes**
>
> The idea is that any member of a team can show leadership.
>
> Steve Morris, Graham Wilcocks and Eddy Knasel, *How to Lead a Winning Team*

This doesn't necessarily mean that one "leader" can't perform both roles, in fact most of the literature you'll read about leadership claims that a leader must do both. That's not necessarily true. Two or more people can share either one of the roles together.

Task leadership is oriented towards expertise, activities and decisions needed to accomplish results, which are measured through productivity. The task leader is concerned with making sure that the team gets the work done.

Maintenance leadership is concerned with communication within the group, and the interactions that generate feelings of group identity, status, attractiveness and personal satisfaction as measured through group cohesion. The maintenance leader is concerned with the relationships and cohesiveness of the team.

So, while you may have a designated leader in your team, you may also find that within the team, there are people who jump to fulfil these roles. The people in the team who initiate activity are the task leaders. The people who are supporting and encouraging are the maintenance leaders and, generally speaking, this role will emerge after the task leaders.

The potential for trouble is when one of these roles outweighs the other. If you have too little maintenance leadership, then everyone will be running off into their own corner to get work done, and your team will feel more like a bunch of individuals rather than a team. On the other hand if you have too little task leadership you'll have a group of people who get along, have nice cozy conversations, but don't get too much work done. The key is to balance these two roles.

When groups first get together, there must be a period of development as the two roles emerge. During this development period, the group will per-

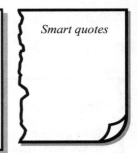
With some [dinner party] hostesses you all talk across at one another as entirely separate individuals, pleasantly and friendly to be sure, but still across unbridged chasms. While other hostesses have the power of making you all feel for the moment related, as if you were one little community for the time being. This is a subtle as well as a valuable gift. It is one that leaders of men must possess.

Mary Parker Follett

form poorly. Let's relate this to the four stages of development described in Chapter 2:

- *forming* – the team is getting together. Task-oriented people are trying to work out what the task is meant to be. Maintenance-oriented people are testing the water, exploring what behavior is allowed.

- *storming* – conflict breaks out. Task-people react emotionally to the demands of the task, and attempt to structure the group in pursuit of different goals. Maintenance-people try to sponsor conflicting rules of behavior.

- *norming* – the team starts to focus in on an agreed view of what their purpose is. The initial task leaders have emerged, and are sharing information openly (those who bid for the role and lost may be in a sulk). The team develops a sense of cohesion as the maintenance function becomes established.

- *performing* – the team is working well. Task and maintenance roles are in balance. There is agreement on how the task should be tackled, and solutions start to emerge. Individuals can integrate their own functional roles with others, as the maintenance function has become established.

While these roles may develop within the team, there's no stopping a leader from ensuring that the team doesn't lose it along the way, and keep them on track.

The adaptable leader

What does this mean for the smart leader? You must be sure that you can adapt your leadership role according to the needs of the situation and the team members. For example, you have a team that is taking on some new work, in an unfamiliar area. You as the leader will need to give them structure and initiate the activity, pointing them in the right direction. But, as the team gets more experienced, you can back away, and start to build the group into a team, opening people up to each other's ideas and opinions or trying to resolve conflict if it arises.

What matters most is that you are able to recognize when there is a gap, and are flexible enough to fill it.

What this doesn't consider is the individual. We have John Adair, the British leadership writer and practitioner, to thank for reminding us of the individual. He developed the idea of *action-centered* leadership which asserts that leaders need to focus on the three "core responsibilities":

- achieving the *task*

- building and maintaining the *team*

- developing the *individual*.

Adair maintains that there will be times when one responsibility would need more attention over the others. For example, when you are approaching a tight deadline, the smart leader will focus on the task and forgo the team night out until the deadline is reached. But that over the long-term these three core responsibilities must be balanced if a leader is going to manage a team effectively and successfully. The appeal of Adair's model is that it's simple and easy to remember. But the other smart bit is that it's not just about the task; the people matter as well. And it reinforces the idea that smart leaders must be adaptable and focus on different "core responsibilities" at the appropriate times.

> Smart things
> to say about teams
>
> It's the ability to be agile
> that counts.

Understanding "group processes"

Keeping teams together and dealing with the potential problems that can arise from a bunch of people interacting isn't easy. Now that you understand that not only the needs of the task but those of the team and the individual need to be balanced, what else can happen? Groups of people are influenced by a lot of different factors. But in order to lead, either within or from outside the team, you need to have a handle on "group processes." Nicola Phillips, author of *Reality Hacking*, describes them as:

SMART PEOPLE
TO HAVE ON
YOUR SIDE:

ROBERT BLAKE
AND JANE
MOUTON
professors at the
University of Texas
and authors of 13
books including The
Managerial Grid

The Managerial Grid is a framework for understanding types of leadership. Leaders are measured based on their "concern for people" and their "concern for production." Blake and Mouton characterize five different leadership styles according to the varying emphasis on each of the two dimensions. They suggest that the most effective leadership is characterized by a combination of high concern for production with a high concern for people – also known as team management.

- participation

- influence

- decision-making

- group atmosphere

- membership

- feelings

- norms.

Smart leaders take the time to get familiar with the "group processes" that exist within their team.

Participation

One indication of involvement is verbal participation. The things to look out for are the differences in the amount of participation among team members.

- Who are the high participants?

- Who are the low participants?

- Are there are any shifts in participation?

- What about the team members that are quiet, how is it interpreted – as boredom, consent, disagreement? What impact does that have on the rest of the team?

- Who talks to each other and why? What are the possible reasons for this?

- Who keeps the ball rolling and why? What are the possible reasons for this?

Influence

Influence is different than participation. You can be a high participant, but have very little influence.

- Who are the high-influence members?

- Who are the low-influence members?

- Is there any shift in influence? Who is shifting their attention?

- Is there any rivalry in the group? What effect does this have on other team members?

Influence can be positive or negative, either encouraging or alienating. How someone tries to influence can make a great deal of difference as to whether they will be successful or not.

- Is there an autocrat, imposing his/her will on others?

- Is there a peacemaker who quickly supports other people's decisions?

- Does someone appear to have a lack of interest – which actually gets them attention?

KILLER QUESTIONS

- Who are the task- and relationship- leaders in our team?
- Are they balanced overall, or does one role dominate the other?

Do other people in the team recognize what patterns or "group processes" emerge over time when we interact with each other?

- Is there a democrat – trying to get *everyone* included?

Decision-making
Decisions are often made without considering the effect on everyone.

- How are they made in the team?

- Are they "self-authorized", supported by only a couple of members in the group? What effect does this have on other team members?

- Is it the case that the majority rules or is there a consensus?

- Does the team drift from topic to topic? Who is responsible for such topic-jumping?

- Does anyone make contributions which do not get any kind of response or recognition, and what effect does this have on the team member who made the contribution?

Group atmosphere
When a team works together, they create an atmosphere. An atmosphere reveals a general impression – to which the team leader should be sensitive. You can gain further understanding by finding out how team members would describe the atmosphere. People may differ in the kind of atmosphere they like.

- Who prefers a friendly atmosphere? Are there any attempts to suppress conflict or unpleasant feelings?

- Who is more comfortable in an atmosphere of conflict and disagreement? Do any team members provoke or annoy others?

- Are people interested and involved? Is the atmosphere one of work, play, satisfaction, sluggishness or something else?

Membership

Membership can be a major concern for team members in terms of the degree of acceptance or inclusion into the team. Different patterns of interaction may develop which will give clues to the kind of membership.

- Have any subgroups developed? Whether two or three team members consistently *support* or *disagree* with each other – they can still be considered a subgroup.

- Do some people seem to be "in" the team and some to be "outside"?

- How are the people "outside" treated?

- Do members move in and out of subgroups?

Feelings

Because feelings are rarely mentioned, you may have to make guesses based on tone of voice, facial expressions, gestures, or other non-verbal clues to

Smart answers to tough questions

Q: How can the leader keep a handle on things like feelings and group atmosphere in the team if more importantly they need to keep their eye on the bottom line?
A: If you don't watch what is and isn't happening within the team in terms of group dynamics, you run the risk of never reaching your target – it's just as important to manage both the people and the target.

figure out what someone may be feeling. It's also worth noticing if anyone is trying to block expressing their feelings.

Norms

Norms are the ground rules you've established with your team. Some can facilitate team progress and some may hinder it. They usually express the beliefs or desires of the majority of the team members as to what behaviors should or should not take place. They may be clear or sensed by only a few, or completely below the level of awareness of any member.

- Are topics avoided in the team? Who reinforces this avoidance? How do they do it?

- Are team members overly nice or polite to each other? Are only positive feelings expressed? Do members agree with each other too readily? What happens when members disagree?

If you can understand the "group processes" going on within the team, it will make it easier to manage problems that may be holding the team back from being more productive.

Influence and power

One of the underlying assumptions about being a leader (besides being ultimately responsible) is that you have some power and influence over others. Isn't that what you get paid the big bucks for?

At the heart of this is the idea that you are trying to get others to make decisions differently from what they did before. You want them to change their behavior; for example, to stop being miserable about work and to start enjoying it.

Yet, if you have influence over someone you rarely call it that, it sounds too selfish or manipulative. Counselling, guiding or advising are more acceptable words to describe encouraging change. Power and influence aren't seen as "nice" words, but they are the unspoken dynamics that underlie relationships.

Smart people learn to recognize how they influence others and develop their influencing abilities. Alvin Zander describes the following methods of being influential (descriptions modified):

- *giving a reward* – you do something I want you to do, and I'll give you something back, for example, public praise, approval, or a new job.

- *being coercive* – you get punished if you don't do what I want you to do, for example, loss of job security, demotion, or delayed promotion.

- *being an expert* – you listen to me because I have knowledge, based on skill, experience or information that I may have.

- *making oneself attractive and referent power* – I am influential because of who I am and whom I know.

- *legitimate authority* – I'm the boss and you have to listen to me.

- *offering general information* – I offer more or less factual statements to the general public, and you decide what you want to do with it.

The process of influencing behavior does not reside in one person. It resides in the *relationship*.

Harold Leavitt, *Managerial Psychology*

- *changing the environment* – I modify the surroundings in a way that requires you to act differently; for example, increasing the speed of the assembly line so that more widgets per day are produced.

The next question is, how do you know when to use which method of influence. First understand whom you are trying to influence, and how they may react. It's not very smart to try to influence someone who isn't interested in changing their behavior. The power exists in the mind of the person you are trying to influence, not in yours. So you need to understand some of the implications of these methods:

- *Reward* – someone who is motivated by a reward is doing it for that reason only, therefore they'll only do what is necessary in order to get the reward. It's unlikely that you will influence someone to change their beliefs or attitudes using this method of influence.

- *Coercive* – rarely well-received method of influence, and even worse is realizing that people are afraid of you.

- *Expert* – this can backfire: people will do the exact opposite of what you may suggest if they believe that you are using your expertise in your own interest on not on behalf of them or others.

- *Referent* – one thing about referent power is that you may end up being influential without even realizing it or planning to be.

- *Legitimate authority* – because this is based on general practice and comes from the organization; if you don't have the support and approval of superiors, then you have to start worrying.

- *Offering general information* – while a very nice thing to do, it doesn't mean that anyone may actually be interested in the issue at hand.

- *Changing the environment* – another tactic that may not be greeted happily by those you are trying to influence: while you may get what you want, you may have some very unhappy people as well. On the other hand, if it's a change that no one really notices, like piping music into the waiting room so that patients don't realize how long the wait is, it may not upset anyone at all.

Now these questions need to be considered:

- What are you actually capable of doing in the situation? For example, you can't try to influence someone based on your expertise if you ain't an expert. So you need to know whether you have the appropriate "resources" available (expertise, rewards, information, time, skill).

- What kind of behavior will the other person welcome most? For example, if you are trying to influence someone who is used to making

… good leaders exercise a great deal of power and influence, but they manufacture it too; there is not a fixed supply of power in an organization so that it is a zero sum game. Good leaders create more power for everyone who will subscribe to the vision and share it.

Richard Koch, *The FT Guide to Management and Finance*

their own decisions, they will not respond well to being told what to do, no matter what they think or feel.

- What ideas will the other person least likely oppose? The content of what you want the other person to do can help you determine what influence method to use. If you are offering something that will be popular, you can present it in a way that allows them more or less autonomy. But if it's something that they may oppose, you may need to use a bit more pressure.

- What are they least likely to resist? People resist things because they think, for example, that you are deceiving them; you are too aggressive or unclear; that what you want them to do will take too much work; or that they do not have the ability to make the change. In any of those cases, you need to provide the appropriate response; either coaching, as in the latter example, or change the way you are saying things, as in the first example.

Generally speaking, people will resist being influenced if they feel they are being pressurized to do so. It is smarter to assume that people will listen to you when you ask them to do something than to force it on them. Everything has costs and benefits, and when you start to think about who really is to benefit – me, the team, the organization, then you can start thinking about which method is most appropriate.

The moral question is always there, don't fool yourself, people do think about it. Are you being manipulative or are you just managing the situation? You need to define your limits. *Remember that power and influence can be dishonest without any boundaries.*

Empowerment

You cannot consider leadership unless you consider empowerment. Empowerment was quickly and widely grasped in the 1980s by thousands of organizations, probably because many organizations and leaders saw it as a way of growing the pie. Rosabeth Moss Kanter, one of the driving forces behind the empowerment movement proclaims that:

by empowering others a leader does not decrease his power; instead he may increase it – especially if the whole organization performs better.

To many, empowerment is a concept and a way of life rather than a set of management tools. And while many senior managers may talk about empowered work forces, getting it to work can be another story. Before we go there, let's explore the "positive" bits about it first.

Empowerment makes sense. Take a look at the definition: *giving individuals in an organization the power to act on their own initiative but in the interest of the team as a whole.* It's an old idea – the people closest to the work understand it the best, they are the experts, they know what the customer wants because they work with them everyday. And if your team is able to do their job well and create new ideas and opportunities, it certainly is good for you – the leader. Not just because it makes you look good to the rest of the organization, but it will make for a happier team overall, which should, long-term, make your job easier.

Smart answers to tough questions

Q: Why are business leaders always looking for parallels in other walks of life, like conductors or sports coaches?
A: Most people find it hard to accept that leadership is more art than science, and that means there may not be a formula out there to give you the answers every time.

SMART PEOPLE
TO HAVE ON
YOUR SIDE:

DOUGLAS
MCGREGOR
(1906–64)

McGregor was a social psychologist, academic and a central figure in the Human Relations School. He stressed the role of belief in management: that everything stems from the mental models and beliefs held by managers. He is best known for Theory X and Theory Y, central to his book, *The Human Side of Enterprise*, published in 1960.

Theory X was based on the assumption that managers believed: "… that workers inherently dislike work and will avoid it if they can. Because of this dislike for work, most people need to be supervised and threatened before they will work hard enough. The average worker prefers to be directed, dislikes responsibility, and desires security above everything else." It was the traditional carrot and stick thinking: workers were inherently lazy, needed to be supervised and motivated, and regarded work as a necessary evil to provide money.

Theory Y, on the other hand, purported "... that the expenditure of physical and mental effort in work is as natural as play or rest. That control and punishment are not the only ways to make people work, people will direct him/herself if he/she is committed to the aims of the organization. The average person learns, under proper conditions, not only to accept but to seek responsibility. That imagination, creativity, and ingenuity can be used to solve work problems by a large number of employees. And that under the conditions of modern industrial life, the intellectual potentialities of the average person are only partially utilized." He had great faith in what people could do if their potential was tapped.

In the early 1950s McGregor helped design a Proctor & Gamble plant in Georgia. It was built on the Thoery Y model with self-managing teams and, its performance soon surpassed other P&G plants.

McGregor believed that "workers' behavior was a consequence of the nature of industrial organizations, or management philosophy, policy and practice, not workers' inherent nature. It is not people that have made organizations, but organizations which have transformed the perspectives, aspirations and behavior of people."

Although they represent two incompatible ends of a spectrum, just before McGregor died he developed Theory Z, which synthesized the organizational and personal imperatives. William Ouchi went on to develop this idea (and wrote about it in *Theory Z*) by analyzing Japanese working methods, which related very strongly to McGregor's ideas for Theory Z. They include lifetime employment, concern for employees including their social life, informal control, decisions made by consensus, slow promotion, excellent transmission of information from top to bottom and bottom to top with the help of middle management, commitment to the firm and high concern for quality.

There are lots of examples of how empowered workforces have saved money, created new methods of working, or created new markets, like Kodak's Zebra team that turned around their black and white film division. Another example is Xerox. They have introduced X Team status, "a team that has found success by working in empowered ways." Xerox is challenging teams to reflect on the way that they work.

A great example of what an empowered workplace would look like comes from their description of an X Team:

- People know exactly what they are doing. They take responsibility for their work, but also seem to know when it is not theirs to take. They may exchange quite contrary views and ideas as they agree a team approach, but they all seem to agree on where they are going.

- Senior people don't get in the way, and yet they always seem to be there, removing obstacles and opening up new paths. They have made some tough decisions about letting go, and appear willing to trust in that agreement. They encourage creativity and risk-taking – using failure as a learning opportunity and a positive way of moving forward.

- Everyone is keen to learn. They have raw enthusiasm for trying new things.

> ... empowerment ... is people taking responsibility for themselves and the organization. This is a move away from a system in which individuals wait for all decisions from the top, take the safe path, and blame others when things go wrong.
>
> Peter Block, *The Empowered Manager*

But unfortunately a lot of leaders have had "problems" with empowerment. Eileen Shapiro author of *Fad Surfing in the Boardroom*, believes that the problem with empowerment is embedded in the word itself. The threat exists because of the idea that power has to be shared. Shapiro is hitting on something very important here, most people take years to build up their reputation and the amount of power they may have, handing it back down doesn't always go down so well.

Many organizations implemented "empowered work forces," but in many cases control was taken back; partly because powerful teams can be threatening and partly because empowerment is not a concept to be laid down onto an overall organization's structure.

What has happened is that empowerment becomes delegation, and let's face it, that just ain't the same. No one wants your work handed down with a label plastered over it that screams latest management fad.

So what is the first step to empower others? Peter Block, author of *The Empowered Manager* and the major contributor to the growth of empow-

Kanter's key books were *Change Masters* and *World Class*. Her career began as a sociologist and her work still has that slant. She sees her subjects as "mini-societies." She is best known for her contribution to change, but is also partly responsible for the rise in interest of empowerment.

erment, suggests that you begin with yourself. You must first claim your own autonomy, your vision and then live it out. Then you can make it easy for others to do the same.

You can also help others by:

- being a coach, a helper to team members, helping them to achieve their goals and work efforts

- contributing in farsighted judgement that complements the day-to-day expertise of colleagues

- making sure the culture you work in, including and especially your boss, isn't "authoritarian"

Q: Aren't I empowering my employees by giving them some more responsibility?

A: Jawboning about "empowerment" but doing nothing more than mouthing kind words and fine sentiments, or enacting empowerment programs without a fundamental commitment to finding ways to consider decisions jointly, are great ways to ensure that the path of forgone opportunities will be the one that most employees will travel.

Eileen Shapiro, *Fad Surfing in the Boardroom*

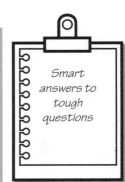

Smart answers to tough questions

And for managers who make the transition [into empowerment], there is a bonus: the opportunity to take part in an expanding scope of decision-making – and to take part in the satisfaction and pride that come from being part of a team that generates and executes more successful ideas than would be possible had their power not been shared as widely. Power-sharing can pay – even for those whose power is shared.

Eileen Shapiro, *Fad Surfing in the Boardroom*

- getting support from your "boss" by redefining what your role will be if you are losing some scope

- getting the appropriate training for your changed role

- making sure the measures by which you are judged and the compensation plan have been revised to reflect your new role

- not talking about empowerment unless you truly plan to implement it, otherwise you'll be setting up false expectations within your team.

But as a leader you can only offer and set the stage for your team members to be empowered – it's ultimately something that only they can do for themselves. And the fact is that not everyone wants to be empowered, some people really would rather follow directions – and that's OK too.

Decision-making

The style of decision-making you use as a leader is a key factor in creating an environment where people have the opportunity to flourish.

Decision-making is one of the core processes of working with your team and, in order to capitalize on the opportunities, it's important that you recognize that there are different levels of participation in decision-making. Each level of participation is appropriate at certain times and in certain situations. Smart leaders know which to go for.

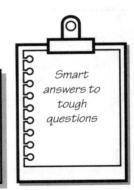

There are five well-known levels of decision-making most of which are modelled after Tannenbaum, Schmidt and Zoll, they are:

- *Level 1 – Tell/Directive:* you tell them what you have decided.

- *Level 2 – Sell/Input:* you ask for input before making a decision. Listen to comments and then you decide.

- *Level 3 – Consult/Dialogue:* discuss the issue fully before you decide. Everybody goes along with your decision.

- *Level 4 – Participation/Ownership/Consensus:* reach a decision that everyone buys into and takes responsibility for.

- *Level 5 – Delegate:* you ask them to decide. They take control.

Q: "Now that I am CEO, what am I supposed to actually do?"
A: "You're supposed to make superficial statements about how good the company is, then hope something lucky happens and profits go up. It's called leadership, sir."

Scott Adams, creator of *Dilbert*

Smart answers to tough questions

If you start to think about when each of these situations might be most appropriate, you may come up with something like this:

- *Level 1 – Tell* – when you are under pressure in a crisis situation (don't say that's every day) or if you have the knowledge and expertise that no one else does.

- *Level 2 – Sell* – when the team is unsure, this is a good time to "sell" your decision to everyone else.

- *Level 3 – Consult* – team members have particular specialist knowledge or expertise to contribute.

- *Level 4 – Participate* – if you're working on a complex or highly pressured project, you'll probably need the input of specialists.

- *Level 5 – Delegate* – when the plan/project is too large or complex to manage on your own, or when you have good sub-leaders and specialists.

These are just guidelines to help you see when it may be appropriate to use different styles. You have to judge and know your team well enough to know which is appropriate at which times.

At the "lowest level" (level 1) if you are using a "directive" style, be aware that the way in which you tell them what to do will have an effect on others' commitment and motivation towards that decision.

At the other end of the spectrum (level 5), where everyone makes decisions together or you delegate the decision to the team, make sure that you are kept informed of progress and what is happening.

Secure their commitment – you just might get creativity

The more people feel included in making a decision, the more committed they will be to making it happen. I know it takes more time to get a commitment, but when a team works together to make a decision, it is more likely to take a wider range of options and possibilities into account.

Even though participatory decisions take longer, those decisions are likely to be more creative. They consider more information, are more flexible and, as individuals gain more knowledge from the debate, they are better positioned to handle unexpected consequences and unpredicted problems without feeling confused or paralyzed into inactivity.

> *Smart quotes*
>
> My role is that of a catalyst. I try to create an environment in which others make decisions. Success means not making them myself.
>
> Ricardo Semler (CEO, Semco)

Don't dump it on them

As difficult as it may seem to believe, individuals can feel empowered by decisions made at any of the five levels. How do you make that happen?

Empowerment is more likely to happen if you provide explanation and consideration rather than just handing down an edict. Then it's important if everyone behaves "appropriately."

For example:

	Leader's behavior	Team member's behavior
Level 5 Delegate	Explain the criteria which decisions must fulfil.	Accept responsibility for decision-making.
Level 4 Participate	Participate and acknowledge the consensual process.	Work on the outcome until it feels right. Commit to the decision.
Level 3 Consult	Listen to and constructively discuss team members' input. Then make the decision.	Actively participate, voice opinions. Support final decisions.
Level 2 Sell	Listen to input. Make the decision.	Voice opinions when asked.
Level 1 Tell	Give a direct command.	Listen and act sensitively and constructively.

You may look at this and say "I can hold up my end of the bargain, but what about the team members?" There are a number of crucial elements that need to be developed and established within the team, before any of the above can start happening, all of which, by the way, builds on the last three chapters.

Smart answers to tough questions

Q: How do I get a team motivated enough to take on more responsibility if all they want to do is "punch in and out" and get their paycheck?
A: Not every team is interested in taking control and making decisions, you need to recognize with whom you're working, and whether there is any potential among those clockpunchers.

Mutual trust and respect

This is true when team members assume that everyone else will be giving his or her best and that everyone intends to be constructive. Individuals' needs, agendas and preferences must be taken into account.

Accessible information

When people work together, they need complete information. Only when they are fully informed will they be in a position to make effective decisions. Information should flow freely, not be held onto or covered up from certain people, or at certain levels. If you can't tell people everything, you may need to consider carefully which level of decision-making is appropriate.

Sharing control

People want to be involved in deciding how they will achieve their goals and reach decisions about which processes will work for them. This means it will take longer to get things started, but it builds complete agreement and commitment to the achievement of the best results.

Shared responsibility

This is true when people are mutually committed to achieving results and correspondingly to sharing rewards, credit or criticism.

Development of skills

Individuals need to have the skills that enable them to contribute fully. This increases their confidence and competence and enables you (the leader) to feel more relaxed about their level of contribution. People need to be given opportunities to learn and develop so that they can be true partners in decision-making processes.

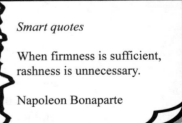

Smart quotes

When firmness is sufficient, rashness is unnecessary.

Napoleon Bonaparte

Facilitation

It's inevitable that, if you are the team leader, people will often look to you for the answers. Questions like, "what kind of scope do we have?" need to be answered. That's not to say that there may not be a lot of good participation from the rest of the team. There will be plenty of times when it isn't appropriate for you to have the answers. Generally speaking the people closest to the "task at hand" know what's best. Therefore, another useful leadership skill is to be able to facilitate discussions/meetings. It's a supportive role, and you'll be working on the barriers that exist between people and helping to build relationships. The idea of facilitation is to assist other people to understand and work through their own issues rather than "fixing it" for them.

Peter Senge describes the role of the facilitator in *The Fifth Discipline* as "the one who holds the context of the dialogue." While Senge's dialogue sessions go "deeper" than just a regular team meeting, because they aim to suspend all assumptions of participants, he has some good points about being a facilitator. They are:

- helping people maintain ownership of the process (how things are happening) and the outcomes – so they can say and believe "we are responsible for what is happening"

- keeping the discussion on track and moving.

Senge quotes Edgar Schein, for a very fine description of the facilitator. "The facilitator walks a careful line between being knowledgeable and helpful in the process at hand, and yet not taking on the 'expert' or 'doctor' mantle that would shift attention away from the members of the team, and their own ideas and responsibilities."

It means not having the answers and allowing team members to work through the issue at hand without mudslinging. Many people describe it as an art, probably because there are no simple models or tools to use to help describe it. It means using your intuition and suspending your logic and problem-solving abilities. You need to get behind the words, summarize without changing the meaning and always check that you've got it right. It's very useful on a day-to-day basis as well as in developing consensual decision-making.

Being in a leadership position isn't easy, it takes an astute awareness of yourself and those you are working with. It also means having the ability to step back and let those that can "just do it." This chapter has developed an understanding of what team leadership is and how you can begin to develop the skills and awareness necessary. We've looked at leadership roles within teams – whether the team leader or team members take them up, but that both roles (task and maintenance roles), be present and balanced in order for the team to perform well.

We've took a look at some of the "group processes" that occur in a team, and smart leaders understand and have a handle on these "processes" in their team. Influence and power have a big impact on a team, and learning what method of influence available, is another skill important for a leader.

Empowerment is an important management idea to be aware of, and one way to manage a team. Decision-making and how to go about creating different environments for decision-making is also an important skill and there are choices of style. We end the chapter with facilitation and how sometimes it's better to let other people work through their own issues, rather than trying to "fix-it" for them.

Whatever your role may be, already a team leader, a hopeful, or a team member, this chapter has key ideas that are important to understand how a team works.

5

What to Do when It Doesn't Work

We have met the enemy and he is us.

Walt Kelly

Creating and maintaining a successful team can be hard work. And there will be times when it won't always "work." But these times don't need to bring despair to everyone. There are some common obstacles and occurrences that come up, and ways of removing them without always having to remove yourself or other people. Remember that, as you tackle problems, you are testing and learning about the "processes" that you may or may not have in place.

Not only do teams have troubles with the project and work that they may be facing, but there are times when team membership or leadership isn't right. And even if you do get all the basic elements just right, team mem-

Judge a team by how it handles setbacks. The best way to prove oneself is to deal well with adversity. Lou Bainbridge of DPR Construction calls these "the big rocks in the road. You watch a problem as it comes toward a team. Then you come in and coach the team through a successful resolution." Solving that first big problem makes it's easier for a team to solve the next one: "the other rocks, the ones down the road, aren't as big as people once thought."

Fast Company, December 1998

bers may start to be disruptive. The first step is awareness of what the problems are before you can start to tackle some of these obstacles.

So how do you know if your team is in trouble? Glenn Parker in his book *Team Players and Teamwork* describes the following signs of trouble:

- members cannot easily describe the team's mission

- meetings are formal, stuffy, or tense

- there is great deal of participation but little accomplishment

- there is talk but not much communication

- disagreements are aired in private conversations after the meeting

- decisions tend to be made by the formal leader with little meaningful involvement of other team members

- members are not open with each other because trust is low

- there is confusion or disagreement about roles or work assignments

- people in other parts of the organization who are critical to the success of the team are not cooperating

- the team is overloaded with people who have the same team-player style

- the team has been in existence for at least 3 months and has never assessed its functioning.

Just a few choice signs of trouble, but certainly not all of them. So what now? How do you start to tackle some obstacles?

Work-based problems

Let's start by looking at what I call work-based problems. This is when it is apparent that there are problems with the tasks in hand. It may be that there isn't enough work to go around or that there is too much. It could be a project that's been delegated down without a clear goal set out, and so everyone is just getting on with their bits and pieces. Does it seem that everyone is spinning his or her wheels, nothing is getting accomplished and everyone is just a little too frustrated? What's the best thing to do in any of these cases? Use your common sense and go back to the basics:

- Does the team understand what the common goal is?

- Do we know what our common approach is, and if so is it working for us now?

- Do we have the right and complementary skills within the team to accomplish this job?

- Do we have support from outside the team, if not how do we start getting it?

- Do we have the necessary resources, and if not, can we get them?

Jon Katzenbach and Douglas Smith, authors of *The Wisdom of Teams,* recommend after you've revisited the basics to try the following:

- go for small wins

- inject new information and approaches

- take advantage of facilitators or training

- change the teams membership including the leader.

Going for *small wins* is a good place to start. When you get stuck, it's sometimes hard to see how you are going to get through it. Often a wall can feel like the whole thing is overwhelming, and you may believe "it can't be done." That's why it can be vital to break things down into smaller chunks, making it more achievable and manageable. For example, your goal may be to "cut bugs in a software program to zero." A great-sounding objective, but probably a bit too elusive. If that goal is redefined to "cut bugs by 50% in the next 6 months," then you're talking about something much more achievable and measurable to go for.

Often if you are deeply involved in something you cannot see what the small wins may be: get help if you can't see them. You may need to enrol someone from outside the project to help you see what a small win looks like.

New information and approaches can shine a different perspective on a problem. In fact new information, fresh facts and perspective are a major part of the development of teams. But where do you find this new info? Benchmark studies, internal case histories, best practices, customer interviews are a start. The chances are that if you are working in an organization, other teams have come up against a similar problem or, better yet, a solution to a problem that can be shared, even if the problem isn't identical.

Getting the courage to look outside the team is the biggest obstacle to this approach, and moving against the stuck momentum to look outside it can be tough. Once you get new information or perspective, you need to decide what you are going to do with it. The team needs to address the question "what does this mean for the team's purpose and performance, and how we need to tackle it?" Don't forget you can start looking to outside management for help.

Facilitators and training can provide a wide range of help in getting teams unstuck. Often the problem is around issues of interpersonal conflict, problem-solving, communication and team working skills. But training and facilitation must be translated into actions. An increase in awareness of feelings and interpersonal conflict is great, but it has to be translated into how the team will use this awareness to get a more effective performance.

Changing the team's membership or leader is probably one of the first things that people think of doing. While it may seem like the most obvious approach, it's also one of the "easiest." It's great to think you could scapegoat the problems of the team away by assuming that it's a member or the

Q: We've gone back to the basics and tried to get unstuck, but we still can't make any headway, now what?

A: You may need to recognize that there are times when obstacles just cannot be overcome and you just have to move on, which may mean that things may never get off the ground or that the party is over.

leader of the team that is holding things back, but be careful; that may not be the case. Team membership changes more easily than leadership, but in either case new membership helps only when the team asks the question, "what are we going to do now?" Just a change in personnel doesn't mean things will magically change.

Roles and responsibilities

What happens when you have a lack of clarity about roles and responsibility? You can guess there'll be a great deal of conflict, confusion and aggravation. Some of the most talented people can lose it if they don't know what boundaries they are operating within. It can start to look like a cat fight unless someone makes decisions about who should be doing what. Often it takes management or the team leader to make these deci-

SMART VOICES

Two chefs at a large off-site catering business based in New York were put "in charge" of the kitchen. One was a very creative and talented chef, and didn't like structure; the other was a good cook, not so creative, but very organized. Neither really understood who was responsible for which bits, and because their styles were so different they went head to head all the time. Not only did it affect the way that they worked together, but it affected the rest of the team in the kitchen. Often assistant chefs were unsure of whose instructions they should follow. Both women and the team needed a clearer understanding of their roles and responsibility.

sions, but whatever your choice, be sure that there aren't resentments left that haven't been addressed and dealt with.

Size of the team

What happens when a team is too large? There's the obvious obstacle, like where to get together because of the sheer size of the team; but what about disparate agendas? How can a large group of people manage themselves? Having a team that is too big just doesn't cut it. People get lost, others can feel intimidated, but generally you don't get the best use of everyone, because even if you have strong leader, it's tough to manage a large team. What's the smart solution? Break down into smaller more manageable teams that take different parts of the project. But be sure that you don't head off in different directions. And that means you'll need to maintain lots of communication and co-ordination between teams.

Geography

As we spend more and more time in different offices, states, and countries from our colleagues, maintaining a team takes more and more work. Take the idea that the distance you are from headquarters determines how differently you will act. For example, if you don't expect the boss to be walking in at any time, you may behave differently from your teammates who have the boss on the floor above them. For team members in disparate locations there is the potential that different agendas, goals and cultures will adversely affect your relationship.

In these cases, where geography gets in the way, smart teams need to develop excellent communication channels and systems, and meet as regularly as possible. And keeping the team's eye on the goals and approaches you'll be using to get there is the best way to stop "other agendas" getting in the way.

Resources

Another potential problem for a team is access to resources. Let's face it, if you have enough time and money, then just about anything seems possible. Unfortunately that is not the world in which most of us operate these days. What's the best approach towards managing what you've got?

- Set out in your team approach what the team's expectations concerning resources will be.

- Expect this to change over time and be prepared to ask for what is further needed.

What kinds of issues are we talking about?

- What if we don't have all the skills and knowledge we need on the team?

- What if we need more money?

- Will team members have to split their time between other projects?

SMART PEOPLE
TO HAVE ON
YOUR SIDE:

RICHARD
HACKMAN

Hackman is Professor of Social and Organizational Psychology at Harvard University and editor of *Groups that Work: and Those That Don't*. He has done extensive research, which includes studying over 300 cockpit crews. He believes that teams start out enthusiastically but get disillusioned as they get frustrated by trying to get the support they need.

- Do we have the appropriate resources and access to the office space, computers, phones, meeting rooms we'll need?

- What if there is information we need somewhere else in the organization – do we have access to it?

You may not know the answers to all these questions right from the start because, as we've said, it's impossible to anticipate what may come up as you begin working, but don't take any of this for granted. At the same time don't get fixated on the answers to all these questions. Some answers will have to develop on their own. But do enrol senior members or management into getting you the resources you may need.

Meetings

Team meetings are important because they give you a chance to communicate, get up to date, and review. Most people say they can't stand them, but really like to go to them, it makes them feel "important." But all too often meetings are a waste of time, especially if you end up spending most of the time talking about irrelevant, insignificant stuff, like the game last night, or the latest greatest movie. I'm not saying don't have fun, but make sure you are having fun and not just burning time.

Recognize when your team meeting is over and don't stick to time rules – cover the agenda and move on. *Smart lesson: make the time in team meetings worthwhile, otherwise people can burn out on them.*

A large American regulatory body was having its monthly board meeting. People flew in from all over the country. The meeting was well set-up, the agenda was laid out, and the topics of discussion were covered in half the time that was originally allocated. When the chairman suggested that everyone go off and enjoy the rest of the afternoon, there were gasps throughout the room. Because the meeting had been scheduled to last another three hours, no one wanted to leave. So they stayed and "made up" things to discuss.

Money troubles

Another reason why teams can fail is money. Isn't it true that if you're part of a team and you're all doing the "same work" surely you should be getting the "same pay"? If you don't get rewarded for co-operating with team members, why bother? Unfortunately individual-oriented pay programs continue to prevail. Partly because we have our own set of skills, and partly because our culture rewards individualism. Organizations need to be encouraged and understand that people want to be compensated in some part for team performance before they will implement it. If that happens then the picture won't seem so imbalanced. (See Chapter 6 for more on reward systems).

I *am* not *a team player*

Some people just do not like working in a team. It could be that they prefer to work on their own and get their best work done when there are no distractions from other people. Everyone has a different style of working and everyone needs to recognize these differences. (See Chapter 8 for more on individuals' preferences.)

So the first place to begin is with yourself. You need to let everyone else know what you need in order to work effectively. For example, if you are someone who needs time to think about and digest what has been said, that you don't like to respond until you've had a chance to think about it first. The smart thing for you to do is to tell everyone exactly that. You can say, "I need to go away and digest this first before I can ..." without alienating yourself from the team. And you'll probably have to be a broken record – repeating this over and over again to remind everyone that that's just who you are. You'll also have to make exceptions for everyone else, and from time to time not take that time out to digest information, but to engage when the team needs you to.

OK, how about the star in the team – you know the person who always seems light years ahead of everyone else. Stars are tough to manage, but not impossible. First it takes awareness, for example, you're in a team and you're bored – things don't change fast enough because you see it coming first. What do you do with that energy? Talk to your team leader or boss. Let them know what is happening, then ask them to help you to find ways to channel that energy. It may be that you need a framework that is slightly different from the rest of the team, or a different role within the team. But don't ignore it.

In the end if you really know that you just can't work in a team, then don't – it's no use trying to fit a square peg into a round hole. Let your boss or

Smart
answers to
tough
questions

Q: There's one individual in our team who makes contributions and does his work, but just doesn't seem to be a "team player," he really keeps to himself. What are we supposed to do about it?

A: Being a "team player" doesn't come easily to everyone. Check to see if your own "eagerness" to be a part of the team is getting in the way. And as long as he/she is pulling their load and is involved at key times, recognize that everyone has different acceptable levels of involvement.

team leader know that you are not a team player and that you don't work well in a team environment.

It should be noted that you could get yourself into trouble if you throw down the gauntlet and proclaim that you just can't work in a team. Make sure that there isn't something else going on – be sure that you're not being disruptive.

KILLER QUESTIONS

Can we be sure there really is a "problem" with our team leader or is it just because we don't always agree with his/her views?

Team leadership problems

People love to say "This isn't working because we have such a lousy team leader." It is *the* bandwagon that everyone feels compelled to jump on. There are times when it is just an easy excuse and convenient. But it can mean that the team isn't taking responsibility for its problems. I'm not saying that team leaders aren't obstacles sometimes, just be careful.

Here are some examples of "poor team leadership":

- *no vision or direction* – a leader who is unable to give the team direction will make team members flounder or retreat into individual jobs/tasks/roles, and ignore the team goals. This will fragment the team.

- *non-specific goals* – a leader who creates goals that are too lofty or general can leave the team feeling depressed and frustrated.

- *doesn't buy into teamwork* – if your team leader doesn't believe in teamwork, then the team can feel dislocated from the rest of the company and unsure of their contribution, creating conflict with other teams and management.

- *disruptive leadership* – leaders can be disruptive in an otherwise functioning team by trying to control too much or meddling in areas that are performing well, or by subverting individuals in the team away from the team project and onto pet projects. On the other hand an aloof leader, who doesn't interact with the team, doesn't praise or recognize the team's achievements can completely de-motivate a functioning team.

- *leads the team in a different direction from the company strategy* – this creates torn loyalties for people in a team and may make it impossible to work well if the goalposts are changing. Individuals may feel isolated and frustrated.

- *leads from too far in front* – the great dynamic visionary leader who leaves his team behind because he moves too fast or may not be able to get the team to buy into his or her vision.

Smart quotes

Bosses are no longer customers, they are suppliers.

Peter Block, *Stewardship, Choosing Service over Self Interest*

I learned firsthand how critical a sense of mission – or its absence – can be to an employer. Several years ago, I had an assistant who handled the arrangements for my speeches and travel; at night she did volunteer work for a non-profit, self-help organization. Her work for me was acceptable but perfunctory. It was clear that she was much more involved and committed to her unpaid work. Frankly, I was jealous. I came to resent the fact that I was not getting her best efforts; after all, I was paying her and they weren't. We talked about it, and she was very honest about the fact that it was her volunteer work that had real meaning for her; there she felt she was making a difference. So you can't expect every employee to be zealously committed to your cause. But you can accept the fact that part of the responsibility for uninspired work lies with the leader.

Warren Bennis

Smart quotes

What do you do in any of these situations? As with any problems or obstacles, you need to talk. Talking through obstacles is important even though it may be uncomfortable, especially if you feel that you aren't getting anywhere. People need to get information about how their behavior is impacting others. Most of the time our biggest problem is that we are just not aware of how we affect others.

A team of programmers at a software company had a team leader (Tom), who was very withdrawn from the team. When there was a problem, he created systems that usually didn't work. When the team questioned him, he obviously felt threatened and retreated even more. Throughout their frustration the team was talking among themselves about what a "terrible" leader they had, he didn't seem to care, wasn't interested, and couldn't figure anything out. When they finally reached a crisis that they couldn't overcome, the team members decided they needed to have a meeting and told Tom that things had to change. They let him know that it wasn't about getting rid of him as team leader, but they needed to figure out how to operate better.

The manager of the department to which the team reported facilitated the meeting and they learned an awful lot. As they started talking through some of their problems, Tom admitted that he recognized what needed to be done most of the time, but that he wanted to do it on his own. The rest of the team were very upset and asked not to be ignored, but to be involved, to know what was going on. They started talking about specifics, but hung it on tasks rather than on individuals (which de-personalized it).

Tom had to face up to problems and what he disliked more than anything – "touchy feely" stuff. He finally admitted that he thought his role was to fix things – but he couldn't always do it. The team were relieved, they let him know that they wanted to know when he couldn't "fix" things, and that it was OK if he could do x, y or z or nothing at all. Not only did Tom need to face up to some uncomfortable feelings about his abilities, but the team needed to make him feel safe in doing so. Everyone had become "stuck" in their perceived roles; once they shook things up, it was easier to get out of entrenched positions.

Talk about it

One of the greatest obstacles to overcome within a team is that it's tough to talk about how you feel. Many problems that teams have are because people aren't always sure how to express themselves.

Let's return to communication and look at the content, or as previously defined, our thoughts and feelings. If thoughts are what we imagine, re-member or reflect on, then feelings are the emotional reactions we have to thoughts including our own and others. For most people in the work place, thoughts are much easier to put your finger on, while feelings and emo-tions are more difficult to understand, and to express. It's true – you don't usually see people gushing with emotion at the office and, when you do, most of us think it's because "something" has happened.

Kolb, Rubin and McIntyre also argue that you can try to "disassociate" your thoughts from your feelings, but that is not smart in the long run for either your ability to communicate or your stress levels. Thoughts and feelings are an important part of expressing yourself and getting your point across. Without feelings and emotions, we would be a world full of an-droids. And the ability to differentiate between thoughts and feelings is an

Smart quotes

Generally speaking, our facility to express, hear and work with thoughts is much greater than our facilities with feelings. What is rational, concrete, objective, and quantifiable seems easier and safer than anything emotional. Feelings are considered "touchy," "too personal" and something "we don't talk about, especially in business." Yet feelings are another component of ourselves. Feelings are the way we personalize our thoughts, ideas and reactions …

David Kolb, Irwin Rubin, James McIntyre, *Organizational Psychology, An Experiential Approach to Organizational Behavior*

important communication skill, and one that is particularly important when you start to deal with obstacles.

But what happens when you do have a team trying to sort out differences and get over obstacles? Usually one of two things, either there is very little interaction and participation, or there's too much. Which is most productive? It may seem that when "all hell breaks loose," you aren't getting much done.

Harold Leavitt uses the term "noise" to describe the static that gets stirred up and interferes with the communication of "really relevant" information.

So you've got two choices, either set up a system where "noise" isn't allowed, for example, a meeting where no personal feelings or emotions are brought up, so that this is a meeting of facts only. Or, as Leavitt proposes, let it all come out. He says it's easier to convert chaos into system than to cover it with system. And most of the time, he's right. If you cover it with system, like anything that gets buried, you don't know what you may be missing or how rotten it might smell once it does come up.

So keeping the channels open gives you the opportunity to bring up everything, as long as it "gets tagged." So if you are going to deal in personalities, go ahead, but someone needs to point out that that's what's happening. That's the smart but tough part, reaching the point where you can identify what's happening, without getting defensive or feeling offended.

Levels of communication

It takes a while for a team to get to the point where you can say what you feel. But moving beyond facts develops relationships further. Jumping into conversations where you talk about how you feel can be inappropriate at times. Everyone has a "level of communication" at which they are prepared to operate. In order to develop relationships, we must move up, in order, through the five levels. They are:

KILLER QUESTIONS

If we continue to give each other different or conflicting information, how can we, in our right minds, expect to provide real customer service?

- *Level I – ritual and cliché.* These are the conversations you have over the coffee machine or water cooler. It's the same conversations with generally speaking the same kind of responses. You don't go too deep, for example, "some weather we're having" or "how about that Knicks game last night?"

- *Level II – facts and information.* At this level you are talking about the tasks in hand and sharing information. It's where we spend a lot of time at work interacting with each other.

- *Level III – ideas and judgements.* This level starts to put a personal slant on things. Also an area where you spend a great deal of time at work, although it is a bit riskier than Level II because your personal ideas and judgements are starting to come through.

- *Level IV – feelings and emotions.* At this level you begin to share and exchange information that relates to how you feel. For example, "how did you feel when Bob cancelled the meeting the other day?" This level can be threatening unless you have first moved through the other levels.

- *Level V – values.* At this level you are now talking about things that motivate you and what is important to you as an individual. It's impossible to get to this level unless you have moved through the first four. It wouldn't make sense to most people if you started talking at this level without having moved through the other four levels with them.

As David Kolb points out, sharing feelings in the workplace is not comfortable, and difficult for a lot of people. Don't expect team members to jump straight into a conversation with, "I felt upset because we didn't achieve …" – be patient and also realize that you may not get there with everyone. It also may not be appropriate: it's important only if the kinds of tasks you get involved in lend themselves to dealing with feelings up-front.

As for sharing values and beliefs, don't expect to get there with a whole lot of people in life in general. Because values and belief systems concern your motivation and what's important to you in life, it's impossible to share this with more than a very small number of people. Also if you start throwing

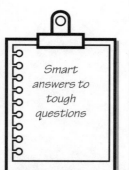

Smart answers to tough questions

Q: It is very difficult to share news in this organization. If you do, you are perceived – no, you are told that you are not "on the team." It makes me believe that sharing information, particularly painful information, with people outside one's own team is a risky endeavour. Can this be right?

A: It shouldn't be. If you end up filtering or editing information because of distrust it will ultimately undermine the ability of the team and the organization to adapt.

out your values at people who don't really know you (i.e., haven't gone through the first four stages with you), then you're going to look like the loony on the bus. It's pretty irrelevant to them if for example, you believe in reincarnation.

Conflict

To most people, conflict is uncomfortable. It comes about because we all have different values, opinions and definitions of the world. Facing up to these differences means uncomfortable conversations and admitting that you don't see eye to eye with someone. It can sometimes bring out the worst in us. But avoiding conflict will definitely stall you. If you don't face the issues that are creating the conflict, you will never move beyond that point.

Alvin Zander in *Making Groups Effective* describes conflict as "if two or more parties disagree over what the other ought or ought not do – when each side *knows* what should be said or done and *knows* that opponents' views on these matters are wrong." He says that friction is more likely to occur when:

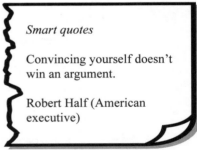

Smart quotes

Convincing yourself doesn't win an argument.

Robert Half (American executive)

- members are rivals rather than co-operators

- the team has no regularized procedures for its activities or for dealing with conflict

- members must share resources that are in short supply

- members are disposed to distrust the intentions of colleagues.

Zander also says that if interpersonal conflict goes on without anyone stopping it, then it will go through several stages:

- members will recognize that they disagree

- opponents will try to confront and persuade one or more of the other members to come on their side

- everyone will get more attached to their initial positions and more eager to defend themselves

- hostility will then escalate on each side

- each side now wants to win and not work toward an acceptable answer

- neither party trusts each other

- tension will then begin to fade because the arguers can't maintain such a high level of emotion for so long

- bystanders will make it clear that the disagreement is unpleasant to them

- participants will then become willing to listen to others not involved in the dispute

- and finally, the arguers become able to reason.

Sometimes it's a long cycle, and takes a while before you reach the last stage. But what good can really come of conflict? If it is "useful" conflict, it can provide a way of finding the best resolution to a problem, i.e., generating more ideas; and it allows you to openly evaluate each other's ideas.

And if your team is encouraging this airing of views, it should mean participation by everyone.

There are ways to work through conflict and here are some steps to talking it through smartly:

KILLER QUESTIONS

Why is there no conflict at this meeting? Something is wrong when there's no conflict. (Michael Eisner, CEO, Disney)

- identify the issues involved

- try to put the issues into a framework that everyone can understand

- look at what the likely cause of the conflict is

- get everyone to identify with the other's point of view

- negotiate compromises or contracts.

Be careful not to blame or criticize. What you are after is to change the way people are behaving, and to influence and be influenced by each other. And ultimately to find a conclusion that everyone can accept.

Warren Bennis writes about the mediation model for resolving conflict devised by Bob Taylor, leader of Xerox's Palo Alto Research Center. Taylor would eliminate the win-lose element from arguments and push for clarification. He urged people to move from what he called a Class 1 disagreement, in which neither party could describe the other's position, to a Class 2 disagreement, in which each side could articulate the other's stance. He not only pushed people to see things from the other person's perspective, but he made them say it, which confirmed whether they really had absorbed and digested that different perspective.

SMART VOICES

Mary Parker Follett was a woman ahead of her times. Indeed her thinking ran counter to the ethos of the time. Follett was a humanist at a time of mechanization. Most of the thinking at the time was of Scientific Management, not the study of human relations. Her philosophy was of interrelatedness – "all people are linked together through evolving relationships in which differences serve as the fuel for the creation of the new." She believed that confrontation and integration of desires was vital and leads to the continuous growth of the individual and the group. She believed in "power with, rather than power over." That confrontation and integration of desires mean a freeing-up for both sides and increased total power or increased capacity.

Follett believed that conflict was a fact of life and that it should be used to work for us; that the only positive way forward was to integrate conflict. To achieve this you must first "uncover" the real conflict and then take the demands of both sides and break them up into their constituent parts. We shouldn't think that resolution only comes when it's an "either-or" situation, this limits our thinking. Often there is the possibility of something better than either of the two given alternatives.

In her book *Dynamic Administration*, which was published after her death, she said "I think we should undepartmentalize our thinking in regard to every problem that comes to us. I do not think we have psychological and ethical and economic problems. We have human problems, with psychological, ethical and economical aspects, and as many others as you like."

Rosabeth Moss Kanter says about Follett, "Follett sent one principal message: relationships matter. Underpinning all of her work is the importance of relationships, not just transactions in organizations. She pointed to the reciprocal nature of relationships, the mutual influence developed when people work together, however formal authority is defined." She was, it could be said, a great advocate of teamwork. Follett was largely ignored by the West, but honored by the Japanese.

If you work through conflict positively you will:

- give everyone the chance to be heard

- enrich the team with ideas

- remove a barrier to communicating and working together

- release a lot of tension that's been building up.

Let's be clear, if conflict arises because of a particular work issue, then talking it through and seeing it from each other's point of view can be incredibly constructive. But if you are in a deadlock because of personality conflict, and you don't identify that there are personality differences, you don't have much chance of moving forward.

Most teams have a hard time facilitating themselves through conflict. Mainly because they are usually too close to the issues at hand, and/or

> Contrary to popular myth, great teams are not characterized by an absence of conflict. On the contrary … one of the most reliable indicators of a team that is continually learning is the visible conflict of ideas. In great teams conflict becomes productive … in mediocre teams, one of two conditions usually surrounds conflict. Either, there is an appearance of no conflict on the surface, or there is rigid polarization. In the "smooth surface" teams, members believe that they must suppress their conflicting views in order to maintain the team – if each person spoke her or his mind, the team would be torn apart by irreconcilable differences. The polarized team is one where managers "speak out," but conflicting views are deeply entrenched. Everyone knows where everyone else stands, and there is little movement.
>
> Peter Senge, The Fifth Discipline

Smart things to say about teams

people in the team may feel that whomever is trying to facilitate has his or her own "interest at heart." That's why it's so useful to have a third party around.

Alvin Zander says that "members of most 'groups' are more inclined to maintain harmony and more interested in removing conflict rather than encouraging it." And the best way to foster harmony is by:

- ensuring that members agree about goals

- selecting recruits who are similar to members in their beliefs and values

- selecting recruits whose skills and aims are relevant to the group's purposes

- ensuring that members accept and conform to the group's standards

- ensuring that members have a desire for group success.

MARY PARKER FOLLETT ON CONFLICT

...conflict ... we cannot avoid, we should, I think, use it. Instead of condemning it, we should set it to work for us. Why not? What does the mechanical engineer do with friction? Of course, his or her chief job is to eliminate friction, but it is also true that he also capitalizes friction. The friction between the driving wheel of the locomotive and the track is necessary to haul the train. The music of the violin we get by friction. We talk of the friction of mind on mind as a good thing. So, in business too, we have to know when to try to eliminate friction and when to try to capitalize it, when to see what work we can make it do. We can set conflict to work and make it do something for us.

It all comes back to the basic needs of Chapter Two – what makes a team. But be smart, remember that conflict, when handled positively, can work for you.

Disruptive behavior

I mentioned to a friend of mine that I was going to be writing about disruptive behavior and she said to me, "for what age group?" As soon as she said it I realized why the idea seemed so uncomfortable. As adults we don't expect to refer to ourselves in that way. But the truth is that all of us have the potential to be disruptive, especially when we are working with other people. Uncomfortable as it may sound, a smart person understands disruptive behavior and how to deal with it. Unlike the conflict that was discussed above, disruptive behavior is not constructive; it threatens the functioning of the team.

So what does disruptive behavior look like? Some examples include:

- talking over other team members

- changing the subject

- laughing at other team members or their contributions

- using inappropriate concepts or jargon

- being dismissive of other team members

- talking about irrelevancies

- withdrawing from the group.

If you are in a team that suffers from any of these examples, you know that it can threaten the effectiveness of the team. If one team member starts to disrupt things by being dismissive of other team members' contributions or by changing the subject, especially to turn it back on their own expertise, it can really turn other people off and frustrate a team, making it virtually ineffective.

The first step in dealing with disruptive behavior is preventive – establish strong team structures and processes. It's harder to disrupt a team that is well structured, or one that has strong "group processes," but if the team's structure is weak, then effectiveness and performance can be reduced to virtually nothing. Even if you do have strong team structures and processes, team members can still disrupt the team's work.

If a member or members can be disruptive regardless of your structure and processes, then the next step is to understand why someone may be disruptive. Nicola Phillips, author of *Reality Hacking*, helps out when it comes to understanding and dealing with someone who is disruptive. A major cause of disruption is because team members may get a sense of exclusion from the group. And, as discussed in Chapter 2, being included is a strong motivational force for many of us. So if the threat of being excluded exists, it can drive people to behave in the worst ways (see *The Abilene Paradox*). Feeling excluded can be the result of many causes including:

- *alienation from the team* – because you don't know what the team's processes and rules are, or because of cultural differences

- *disagreement with team goals* – because you think the team has misunderstood their brief or that it is out of step with the organization's policy

- *misunderstanding the team's goals* – because of a bad briefing about the team's objectives, or a language problem

- *not being able to understand what is being said* – there's too much technical jargon or real language difficulties

- *not understanding why you are there* – usually occurs because there was no briefing and you don't understand your value to the team

- *not being able to get your point across* – the team is ignoring its "group processes," and there is an uneven distribution of contributions

- *not being able to get your own way* – in terms of work or personal objectives

- *lack of interest in the team's task or goals* – there are a number of different causes, because you'd rather be somewhere else; a lack of confidence; or the feeling that your contribution is not valued

- *feeling that the team's goals are out of line with the organization's* – this may take the form of criticism of either the team or the organization being out of step.

Generally speaking, people who are disruptive are trying to regain control that they feel that they have lost by being excluded.

A common reaction to feelings of exclusion is defensiveness. If a team is faced with an uncomfortable issue and team members feel that they could be excluded or vulnerable, usually the first reaction is to avoid the issue, without even being aware that they are avoiding it.

THE ABILENE PARADOX

Jerry Harvey, author of *The Abilene Paradox and Other Mediations on Management*, tells the story of a visit to his family in Texas. On a hot July afternoon, the Harvey family was sitting in their Texas house playing dominoes. The heat was made tolerable by a fan on the back of the porch; the group had cold lemonade to drink; and the game of dominoes represented the correct level of intellectual and physical effort needed on such a day. Suddenly, however, Harvey's father-in-law said, "Let's get in the car and go to Abilene and have dinner at the diner." Abilene was 53 miles away and they would have to travel in an un-airconditioned car. Jerry thought, "Why travel that far in this heat to eat in that diner?" But, because his wife jumped in saying, "Sounds like a great idea," Jerry found he was unable to display his actual feelings. He tried to show some reservation by saying that his mother-in-law might not want to go, which she of course, quickly denied.

They made the trip and it met their worst expectations. The heat was stifling, the food was appalling and four hours later everyone returned home, hot and exhausted.

Once the mother-in-law admitted she would have rather have stayed home, but felt pressured to go along because everyone else was so enthusiastic, the truth began to come out. Jerry admitted he wasn't interested at all, but felt he was going to satisfy everyone else. His wife said she expressed enthusiasm because she wanted to be sociable and keep the others happy. The final blow came when his father-in-law admitted that he never really wanted to go, but thought that because Jerry and his wife don't visit often that they might be bored, and would have enjoyed it.

All four members of the family agreed because they didn't want to alienate themselves from each other.

"Here we were," Harvey recounts, "four reasonably sensible people who – of our own volition – had just taken a 106-mile trip across a godforsaken desert in furnace-like heat and a dust storm to eat unpalatable food at a hole-in-

> the-wall diner in Abilene, when none of us had wanted to go. To be concise, we'd done just the opposite of what we wanted to do."
>
> Egged on by fears of separation and irrational negative fantasies, reasonable, intelligent people will do just about anything – except what they all privately agree they should do.
>
> "The inability to cope with agreement, rather than the inability to cope with conflict, is the single most pressing issue of modern organizations; the fear of taking risks that may result in our separation from others is at the core of the paradox."
>
> Jerry Harvey, *The Abilene Paradox and Other Meditations on Management*

We all develop a range of defense mechanisms to protect ourselves with, in fact we are often unaware that we are being defensive. It's all part and parcel to survival – isn't it? Partly true, but not when that defensiveness starts to hamper your ability. Typical defense mechanisms include and may sound like:

- *denial, or rejection of information* – "That's not true, I'm never like that."

- *blaming others or circumstances beyond your control* – "It wasn't my fault. They all left me with it."

- *lying* – "I never got any of the relevant information."

- *agreeing too quickly* – "Yup, you're right, I know that, I'll try it your way tomorrow."

- *changing the subject* – "Well it's not getting the contract that's important, it's the fact that I wasn't told about the change of plan."

People employ different defense mechanisms for different reasons, everyone has their own style that they find works for them in different situations. Trying to understand what element of oneself someone is trying to protect can be very difficult, it's very hard to know how central to self-concept someone's behavior may be.

Dealing with disruptive behavior

So what's important then about dealing with disruptive behavior? You must first decide who is best to deal with it. Generally speaking this is something that is best left in the hands of the team leader. That doesn't mean that a team member isn't capable of handling it. You may find that a team member can see the disruptive behavior more readily; if that's the case, then it should be pointed out to the team leader if it's not appropriate for the team member to deal with.

After it's been decided who will tackle the disruptive team member, look at the defensive pattern that someone chooses – it can tell you a lot about him or her. But remember the way you deal with it can tell a lot about you too. Defensive behavior indicates that something very precious is perceived to be under attack. But remember that dealing with disruptive behavior is not a situation where someone "wins." Disruptive team members don't need to be conquered they need to be understood. It useful to step back from the situation, try and detach yourself from the arguments that may be happening and to act calmly. It also means listening more carefully. Evaluating the situation before you deal with it is key. You need to ask yourself the questions:

- When were the defense mechanisms aroused?

- What has happened to activate them at this stage?

- How much is the individual relying on their defense mechanisms in order to function normally at this point in time?

Once you've evaluated the situation, you can start to think about dealing with it. If you re-frame the defense mechanisms discussed earlier into the following problems, they can then be tackled. Is the disruptive person doing any of the following:

- intellectualizing

- diverting

- externalizing?

KILLER QUESTIONS

How often do we realize that someone is creating a "problem" because they actually feel excluded and we are responsible for making them feel that way? And do we ever try to "bring them back" into the team?

Intellectualizing

This defensive behavior involves thinking and talking about issues in an abstract or theoretical way. It may involve someone using a lot of technical jargon, but in general it means keeping the problem at arm's length. This way the feelings, emotions, and responsibility can be avoided, and the disrupter can talk at great length about an issue without really dealing with it.

Dealing with intellectualization may have to be pointed out to that person. That doesn't mean walking up to them and saying "I think you're intellectualizing the issue, which means you're not taking any responsibility for it."

Expect that one to backfire on you. Instead, you need to tell them how you may be feeling. That could be that you feel kept on the outside, or that there's a lot of talk, but that you aren't getting very far. In doing this you are appealing to the team's task to get around the defense mechanism.

Another approach is to appeal to the team's disposition, by saying "I understand what you are saying, but I don't get the feeling that you are really involved in this situation." The idea behind either one of these tactics is to avoid attacking the disruptive team member and increasing their feelings of exclusion. It also avoids antagonizing other team members. If all else fails, get the team to restate the objectives.

SMART PEOPLE
TO HAVE ON
YOUR SIDE:

ALVIN ZANDER

As a professor, researcher and author studying how groups work and what makes effective groups, Zander is a pioneer in the field of group dynamics. He explores how groups can become more effective, how to become a more effective group member and how group to group interaction can be improved.

He believes that groups need the following four qualities to work more effectively:

- free interaction
- dependency on each other
- adequate group attractiveness
- effective group power

and that creating a more effective group involves the following factors:

- choosing clear and challenging goals
- strengthening the desire for success
- improving the decision-making process
- communicating effectively
- establishing standards
- fostering harmony among group members.

Diverting

Another method of avoiding an issue is either to change or divert the subject or to launch into irrelevant detail, which confuses everyone.

The best way to deal with this kind of behavior is to bring the person back to the point. You can use phrases like "That's definitely true, but I feel we are getting away from the point. Can we just go back to ...." By restating the team's objectives you can bring a disruptive team member back into line.

Externalizing

Someone using an external defense will be blaming someone or something else. It can range from "this is a total waste of time," to mutterings under their breath of "what would they know anyway?" This kind of defensiveness is a lot trickier to tackle than the other two, and demands a great deal of control.

It doesn't make sense to ignore this kind of behavior, because if the defensiveness comes from a feeling of being excluded, then if you ignore it, you're feeding into those feelings of exclusion – and on top of that it doesn't make the comments stop. It's crucial that this team member gets acknowledged, no matter how destructive their comments might be.

So how do you acknowledge them and get them to move on? Whatever you do, don't play the schoolteacher by scolding them. You want to describe what they are doing in rational and active words, without judging them. For example, saying things like "OK, I see what you are saying, let's move on and see what Joe has to say." By doing this you are acknowledging them without judging the contribution.

If they persist, you can then try and turn responsibility back onto them. For example, "you've said a couple of times that you think this is a waste of time. What do you feel we can do to stop that from happening?" By doing this you are acknowledging their comment but also asking them to bring things back around to what is important for the team, it focuses on the team's tasks and norms that are established.

It's very important that you don't make this team member feel further threatened by "giving them a piece of your mind." That could just make things a lot worse.

Confronting disruption

Confrontation is another word that makes most of us very uncomfortable. For some it leaves images of shouting and red faces. Confronting someone's disruptive behavior definitely doesn't mean the above. You don't want to identify or expose someone's defensive behavior. What it does mean is objective, accurate and specific descriptions of what is going on. You want to point out people's defenses rather than to destroy them. And while you may want to respond in a hostile manner to someone who is winding you up or leading you off-track, hostility means you are no longer in control. That's not real confrontation or very constructive. So be smart; remember that when you are dealing with a disruptive team member you should:

- *be calm* – which means not jumping to conclusions or to actions until you've had a chance to get a good idea as to what is behind the disruptive team member's reactions and your own

- *avoid misinterpreting* – make sure that you aren't jumping to conclusions and are leaping in before you know what's happening

- *avoid forcing reactions* – learn from experience. If you react to someone emotionally, acknowledge that you have.

Disruptive behavior is not an easy issue. Whether you're the team member or leader, if you are faced with a disruptive team member, the longer it goes on without being addressed the more ineffective the team will become.

You've now had a chance to take a look at a number of obstacles that your team may face. But, again, the first step in conquering obstacles is having solid team "processes" and structures in place. The stronger the foundation your team is built on, the better chance you have of weathering the storm. And smart teams build on their setbacks, they learn more about each other – and how they can work more effectively together. I'll say it again, it ain't easy, but when it works, it's worth it.

This chapter has focussed on how to recognize when your team is having "troubles." We've looked at "work-based" problems that include things like: not enough resources, understanding roles and responsibilities, and team leadership problems, and how best to deal with them. Conflict has taken up a large section of the chapter and, while it's usually something most of us avoid like the plague, there is a difference – it can be constructive, or disruptive. You should, be able to more readily recognize the difference, and understand how to deal with it to make it useful rather than a road block. The emphasis throughout the chapter has been that talking it through, with an awareness of what is actually going on is the best way to deal with whatever the problem may be, even though it may feel "uncomfortable."

6

Make It So

Talent wins games, but teamwork and intelligence wins championships.

Michael Jordan

Getting results is what most of us get paid for, yet actually getting a desired result doesn't always happen. Maybe because most of us are too anxious and desperate to dive into action and tackle the problem that is staring us in the face. But figuring out if you've gotten anywhere means you need goals to point you in the right direction. Goal-setting, problem-solving, creative thinking and getting support from the outside will set you in the right direction. But so will reflection within the team, stopping and looking at how things have been going, and to answer the question: what now?

Smart quotes

It ain't what you do, it's the way that you do it. And that's what gets results.

Bananarama

Goal-setting

As you know from Chapter 2, goals give your team something to do and having a goal is incredibly important to success in a team. The need to achieve is in all of us, and achieving a goal is the perfect means of fulfilling that need. But before you go about achieving goals, you need to set them, so even before you jump into action, you need to sharpen your pencil. *Goal-setting must happen after you've identified what the problems are and before you take action.* For many people, "solving" the problem becomes the goal, instead of coming up with a plan of action, probably because putting the time and effort into goal setting can be excruciating for some. At the other extreme, you may come across people who are so detail-oriented that they lose sight of the problem. Not good either.

KILLER QUESTIONS

How can we contribute to the bottom line, if we don't even know what we are trying to achieve as a team?

Setting goals as a means of tackling problems

Smart teams set goals that:

- keep you motivated

- keep you on track

- focus your attention on action

- motivate you to look for strategies.

So if you are going to set goals that achieve this, then guess what – you need goals that are SMART:

- Specific

- Measurable

- Activity- and achievement-based

- Realistic

- Timed.

Specific

Specific goals aren't wishes. They are real. Specific goals are a statement of what you want to do and how you want to do it. For example:

- We want to cut delivery times to international clients, so we are going stop using regular mail channels, and start using overnight express packaging.

or

- We need to improve our customer service, so we are going to respond to all customer requests within 24 hours.

Both of these specific goals address not just what you want to happen, but how you are going to do it, a behavior or a pattern of behavior is being described. Take either one of these examples above, put a period where the first comma is, and you have wishful thinking.

> *Smart quotes*
>
> People don't do the wrong thing because they want to do the wrong thing. They do the wrong thing because they're not clear about what the right thing is.
>
> Debra Dunn (Hewlett Packard), *Fast Company*, April–May 1998

Measurable

If you want to know if you are getting anywhere, you need to be able to tell if you've made any progress. For example, just saying that you want to cut down production time. This doesn't give you a yardstick to determine whether you have gotten there or not. But, if you say that you want to cut down production time by 50% by the end of the next quarter you've established something to measure your progress against. Measurable goals need to be quantified in some manner, whether it's numerical or not.

Be careful about putting a numerical measure on everything, for example, relationships. Sure you can decide you want to "get to know your team mates better", and you can be specific by saying that you'll do this by organizing a company dinner once a month. But don't think that you can quantify how well you'll get to know them, for example, that you'll know your team 50% better by the end of the third dinner – what does that really mean? Relationships are rarely quantifiable. You could give yourself a yardstick, a measure by saying that you'd like to know more about who they are outside the workplace, for example whether they have family or whether they have any hobbies.

Activity- and achievement-based

Besides being specific and measurable, goals need to be focussed on the activity and what you want to achieve. That means not focussing on the method of achieving your goal. For example:

- We need to be more assertive with the team leader about our ideas.

Being assertive is the method you would use to get ideas across. But if you focus on the activity and the achievement you would sound like this:

- We need to convince the team leader at our next meeting that our ideas on cutting production costs by 25% should be implemented at the beginning of the next quarter.

You've shifted from a method to an activity, and something that everyone can do some actual work towards. It's also useful to use the past tense (in the example above, the idea implemented), that way you know what you are specifying is a goal and not just the way of getting to that goal.

Realistic

Being realistic isn't always fun. It's much more enjoyable to walk around with a fantasy of what life could be like. But without being realistic not only will you end up frustrated and de-motivated, but you'll never have that fantasy life. A goal is realistic if:

- you have the resources necessary to achieve your goal

- there are no external circumstances preventing you from achieving your goal

- the cost of achieving it isn't too high.

In a team, if even one person can't achieve their own goals, it can de-motivate the whole team. And different people will respond to goals in different ways. The competitive folks probably won't be very supportive, whereas others may be more supportive. Most important is to avoid setting goals that aren't realistic, otherwise watch out for disruptive behaviors and use what you know about "group processes" to stop things from deteriorating.

Timed

You need to have a specific time-frame for achieving goals. If you think you can say "I'll spend two hours a week on customer relations problems as soon as we get a chance," or "when the current push is over" and actually achieve that goal, you've got something coming. It is a great way to procrastinate and better yet a great way to never really achieve it.

SMART goal setting is useful for not only teams, but for individuals as well. So while your team may be good at setting their own goals, each individual needs to use SMART to set their own goals.

When you are setting goals, you also need to think about the costs to the team and to others. If you decided to cut production costs by 50% by the end of the next quarter, what does that really mean for you as a team? What are the costs that come with that decision, and who will you be affecting – does it mean redundancies somewhere, changes in manufacturing partnerships? It's smart and vital to think about the implications of your goal rather than just the benefits.

What else do you need to achieve a goal? Get support from your team leader or manager you may report to by getting him/her to help you to:

- identify what resources and strengths you have available to the team

- mobilize ways of achieving the targets that you've set out

- implement your plan

- evaluate the results.

SMART PEOPLE
TO HAVE ON
YOUR SIDE:

MICROSOFT

Microsoft is incredibly successful at holding on to their staff and producing development teams that work incredibly well together. Their secret – they give their people very clear goals, tell them what is expected of them, and let them get on with it.

Alvin Zander in *Making Groups Effective* suggests that a moderately challenging goal is more beneficial than a difficult or easy one. In order to ensure that the group chooses a challenging goal, team members and leaders should:

- report to members how well the team is doing over time
- clearly define the team's mission and goals
- encourage a desire for group success among members
- play down fear of failure among members
- encourage members to compare the team's score with that of other teams
- try to have outsiders place realistic demands on the team
- improve the team's procedures so they are as efficient as possible, and work to keep them that way.

Attaining goals

Once you've figured out what your goal is, then you can start thinking about attaining it. Three things need to happen next. You need to:

- identify and assess strategies to achieve your goal

- put together a plan of action

- implement the plans.

Smart quotes

The drive to problem-solve is as close to the heart of our species as is language – indeed, language itself may have evolved because of its utility in solving problems.

Warren Bennis, *Organizing Genius; The Secrets of Creative Collaboration*

Having a strategy doesn't mean developing a corporate strategy, this book doesn't go there. It does mean choosing realistic methods of achieving your goals, and looking at ways of dealing with problems that may come up.

Thinking strategically doesn't always come as second nature to everyone, and for those that it does, there are plenty of things that can stop you from attaining a goal. Most of us can come up with lots of outside influences, like not enough resources or support. But many times goals aren't achieved because you can't actually think creatively or strategically. Some factors that you can "control" just by becoming aware of them are your:

- reliance on authority to give you the answers

- stress

- fear.

Reliance on authority
Relying on authority to have the "right" answers is something you probably learned at an early age. And unfortunately this will stop you from thinking creatively. For some, believing that there is no higher authority that has the "right" answer can be tough to accept.

Stress
Hard work and frustration from not being able to solve a problem immediately can create anxiety and stress, which in turn can block creative problem solving.

Fear
How many times have you held back an idea because you were afraid it

would sound stupid or silly? This kind of fear can hold you back, but so can anxiety about the problem and fear that you can't solve it, which *will* stop you from being able to come up with a solution.

Thinking outside your box (or cubicle)

Part of attaining goals is overcoming problems, and being good at solving problems. To solve a problem, you can look at it and say, "hey I've seen this before, let's solve it based on what I know already." Most of the time we try to overcome something by doing what we know already, but trying to do it faster or more often. Many times that's not the solution: turning up the volume doesn't always work.

Generally speaking, you need to look at things from a new perspective. For example, if someone asked you what uses a DVD has. The first thing that pops into mind is that it plays movies or music. While that may be true, and obvious, there are other ways of looking at that DVD.

> *Smart things to say about teams*
>
> The man [or woman] who has no imagination has no wings.
>
> Muhammed Ali

If you look at how the world operates now, with things changing so quickly, no one believes that they have the answers based only on past experiences, let alone believing that there is one right answer. Life is too complicated for that. If we took that DVD and tried to come up with other uses for it, you could use it as a coaster or a Frisbee. The idea is that you must be able to see things, not necessarily for what they are, but from different perspectives. And a different perspective is something that teams have to offer – especially if you are in a diverse team. But harnessing this kind of thinking is not always easy.

Brainstorming

The idea behind brainstorming is to write down as many ideas or thoughts you may have about a problem. The key to its success is to stop you from judging the ideas first, no matter how silly they may sound. You need to stop yourself from saying "yes, but I think …"Once you've got the ideas written down, then you can start clarifying what they mean, and evaluating whether any of the ideas are possible solutions to the problem.

In order for brainstorming to be effective you need to:

• keep the definition of the problem broad

• stop yourself from judging the ideas

• aim for quantity, you want as many ideas up there as possible, no matter how outlandish they may sound

• write it all down so that everyone can see them

• go for one more round of outrageous stuff if you think you've had enough in the first round.

By all means save the judgement for last – don't kill any ideas while they are being developed in the brainstorming session. Brainstorming doesn't tell you what to do with the ideas after you've come up with them, but it's a starting point.

Working in a team gives you more opportunity to make better overall decisions and come up with different ideas than if you worked alone, although it's not impossible to brainstorm on your own. But as Warren Bennis says, with more than one person, "more options are thrown into the hopper."

Lateral thinking

Think about the three astronauts in the fated Apollo 13 flight. In the movie, Ron Howard did a great job dramatizing the five perilous days, after the in-flight explosion that put their lives at risk. But they survived it because they had a great team on the ground that was able to analyze and solve a series of complex technical problems. And some of this meant "thinking outside the box." For example, NASA engineers figured out how to repair the spaceship's damaged air-cleaning system, using only the materials on board.

These engineers were using "lateral thinking." So what is lateral thinking? Developed by Edward de Bono in 1967, he defines it in illustrative form as:

You cannot dig a hole in a different place by digging the same hole deeper.

This means that trying harder in the same direction may not be as useful as changing direction. Effort using the same approach will not necessarily succeed.

> Smart things
> to say about teams
>
> An essential aspect of creativity
> is not being afraid to fail.
>
> Edwin Land (inventor of the
> Polaroid camera)

In lateral thinking, de Bono suggests you are changing concepts and perceptions. You start out with certain ingredients, just as in playing chess you start out with given pieces. But what are those pieces? In real life the pieces are not given, we just assume that they are there. We assume certain perceptions, certain concepts and certain boundaries. Lateral thinking is concerned not with playing with the existing pieces, but with seeking to change those pieces. It is concerned with the perception part of thinking – where we organize the external world into the pieces we can then "process."

Traditional thinking has to do with analysis, judgment and argument. In a stable world this was sufficient because it was enough to identify standard situations and to apply standard solutions. This is no longer so in a changing world where the standard solutions may not work. You must suspend those boundaries and concepts in order for lateral thinking to work. So the NASA engineers had to suspend his/her thinking about what those materials on board where really used for, and thought outside the boundaries of what their "real" use was for.

Helpful or not

Sometimes you may find that you've spent plenty of time working through the SMART goals you want to achieve, you've brainstormed ideas and put your lateral-thinking heads on, you developed a plan of action, but still things seem to go wrong. That's because it would be impossible to anticipate every problem that may arise. So now what?

- Try not to be deterred from carrying on or to avoid unforeseen problems.

- Seek support from outside the team, and within.

- Ask for help from your leader and manager, and bring problems up at team meetings.

Edward de Bono has had a major impact on the way that we think. He invented lateral thinking in 1957, on which he has written 38 books, and is world-renowned. There is a great response to his work across an unusually wide spectrum. For example, in Venezuela, by law, all school children must spend an hour a week on his programs. In the USA, Canada, Australia, New Zealand, the Republic of Ireland and the UK there are thousands of schools using de Bono's programs for the teaching of thinking.

Not only has he had a great impact on school children, but also he has made a big contribution to creative thinking in business. His contribution has been to take the subject of creativity and to put it on a solid basis. He has shown that creativity is a necessary behavior in a self-organizing information system. His key book, *The Mechanism of Mind*, was published in 1969. In it he showed how the nerve networks in the brain formed asymmetric patterns as the basis of perception. From this basis, de Bono developed the concept and tools of lateral thinking. The term "lateral thinking" is now so much a part of our language that it is used equally in a physics lecture and in a television comedy.

Peter Ueberroth, whose organization of the 1984 Olympic Games in Los Angeles rescued the Games from oblivion, attributed his success to his use of de Bono's lateral thinking. So did John Bertrand, skipper of the successful 1983 challenger for the America's Cup yacht race. Ron Barbaro, President of Prudential Insurance (USA) also attributed his invention of living needs benefits to de Bono's methods.

SMART PEOPLE TO HAVE ON YOUR SIDE:

EDWARD DE BONO (1933–)

Another useful way of looking at problems you may come up against is to determine what is helpful and what is preventing you from achieving your goals. The best way to approach this is to put a list together. On one side you list the things that help you, and on the other you list those that are stopping you – same idea as a pros and cons list. Once you analyze a problem this way, it's easy to see what can be tackled.

Team Reviews

Reviewing progress is a valuable tool for teams; it gives you a chance to think about what has happened, how you've worked together and whether you can make any improvements in the future. Often reviewing is something that "we just don't get the chance to do." Things that get in the way include the following notions:

- We're too busy, we don't have the time.

- No news is good news.

- Most of us are more reflective on the way home from work, rather than with our colleagues.

- Reflecting, exploring and examining are just a waste of time.

- It's safer to be "busy" rather than take the risks associated with examining performance and receiving feedback.

- Not wanting to be "critical" of others.

But replaying the events and experiences and looking back at them not only helps you to determine what progress you've made. They can also:

- help to identify the strengths of the individual, team and project

- improve quality and build confidence and clarity of understanding

- recognize the shortcomings of the individual, team and project, which can lead to developing plans to better performance

- look at priorities and how these compare to what you are actually do-ing, i.e., help you focus on what's important

- get you to consider the context for your activities, to ask the question "why are we doing this?" and to put things into the bigger picture.

KILLER QUESTIONS

Can we afford not to review our progress?

Team reviews may be needed for a number of different reasons. For example, you may want to consider:

- progress against the plan

- the effective use of time in meetings

- the effectiveness of interpersonal communication, problem-solving and decision-making processes

- the consequences of different actions or processes

- reviewing co-operation with other teams/departments/divisions.

As you can see, there are lots of opportunities to apply review techniques to get performance improvement. OK, now how do you go about it? These are main areas to focus on:

- *Task – has the objective been achieved?*

  Here you are focussing on the specific objective of the project/job/activ-ity. You are trying to establish whether the task has been completed and how far through completion the group or individuals are against their objectives.

- *Content – what has been learned or decided?*

  The focus here is on the specific learning, knowledge or principles that can be drawn from the project to further individuals' or group understanding of what works and what doesn't, and how this might be applied next time.

- *Process – how has this been achieved?*

  This focuses on the attitudes, behaviors and dynamics of the group and individual contributions. The purpose is to raise awareness of these issues and to improve interpersonal relationships that may be interfering with performance or causing the team to undervalue their potential.

- *Conclusion and application – where do we go from here?*

  The focus is on future actions and ways forward, experimenting or trying things out. You may be setting new targets or objectives: most importantly that these are not happening in a black hole; and that once a decision for action has been made, someone is responsible and accountable for it.

Don't make the assumption that the only time for review is at the end of a project. That's where many of us get into trouble. Reviews can take place

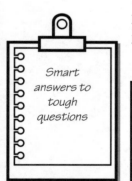

Smart
answers to
tough
questions

Q: Isn't it possible that stopping for a review will mean we lose momentum and direction?

A: Not if you're on the right track. If you are, you shouldn't have any problems gaining momentum back. If you're not – well be happy you stopped – you've saved some time for yourself down the road.

at a number of different times, pre, periodic, spontaneously, or postmortem.

- *Pre-review* – gives you the opportunity to apply learning and conclusions from earlier activities and/or to focus on what you want to achieve – basically it focuses on the planning phase of an activity.

- *Periodic review* – is used at pre-planned times or at fixed milestones. It gives the team the opportunity to stand back and check on progress and how you are operating. It's a vital time for review because all too often we chug along thinking we'll know whether it's right or not when we finish, which isn't always the case.

- *Spontaneous reviews* – this is for when you're just not sure if things are right are not, and need to stop the action and check it out.

- *Postmortem* – rather than this being an opportunity to just reflect on the outcome of the work you've just done and what helped or hindered its progress; it's also a good time to summarize and plan for improvement.

If your team is taking time to establish goals and approaches, you can build in questions about improving performance, and learning from past experiences. Pre- and postmortem reviews are most common, but the problem with only having a pre- and post- is that you don't get to stop yourself midway and say – hang on a second, we need to catch this here and now. *Smart teams stop themselves midway because that's where real insight comes into play,* not with postmortems, where hindsight is 20/20. Stopping midway to review is difficult, it may feel "unnatural" because you may want to follow the momentum you have going. But stopping may mean you will see problems coming before they hit the fan.

A pitfall of team reviews is getting stuck on the numbers (targets met or not) or on "blaming" someone for mistakes or problems. *Reviews are times to learn.* But to review you need to give each other some feedback.

SMART PEOPLE
TO HAVE ON
YOUR SIDE:

THE LETHAL
TEAM AT
QUANTUM
CORPORATION

The Lethal Team at Quantum Corporation developed a "dashboard" to measure performance. The team comprised people from marketing, manufacturing, engineering, quality assurance, finance and human resources. Their goal was to design and build 2.5-inch disk drive, while the company had only ever made 3.5-inch drives. The team leader found out early on that the best way to hit their deadline, which was considerably shorter than any other project, was to detect problems early on.

When they tried to establish a schedule, they soon found out that everyone had different interpretations of what a schedule would look like. For example, many members of the team had sketched out milestones, while others provided a complete schedule for performing tasks. And none of the schedules had been integrated.

Their solution was that instead of using a spreadsheet to measure their performance, they developed a dashboard to display how things were going. Items on the dashboard included a section called Development Status, which measured Product Development as well as Process Development, and Milestones Completed again Milestones Planned. They had a gauge that measured Product Costs in terms of Bills of Materials and another gauge for Overhead.

Lethal was successful in getting potential customers for their new disk drive, and completed the project 33% faster than other teams. They felt that the gauges help them track progress with potential customers, but it didn't help them discover a key problem until relatively late: their test procedures were much more rigorous than industry norms, which made the drive's failure rate appear relatively high. This meant they'd have a hard time selling the product. While the gauges worked well for measuring performance, ultimately, like other measurement tools, they couldn't replace the decision-maker.

Christopher Meyer, *The Work of Teams*

Giving feedback

OK, I'm afraid I am now going to stress the importance of feedback. I know feedback is not something that everyone likes – possibly because it feels like negative remarks, dressed up in a positive way – but quality feedback doesn't have to be a painful experience.

Because feedback is an important part of success and can feel uncomfortable to many people, you must follow the principles of giving and receiving it; this will produce quality feedback. You must also recognize when you are and aren't able to deliver quality feedback. And if you can't then you need to recruit help in facilitating it, or wait until you have perspective on the situation.

So what makes quality feedback? The first and most important principle is that it focuses on behavior and not personality. For example, if I was giving someone feedback about their communication style I would say, "I was upset that a couple of times during our last meeting you interrupted me mid-sentence". Not "I think you don't know how to listen, are rude when you interrupt people and are a loudmouth". The latter is not only insulting, but also name-calling and not constructive, you can see why someone wouldn't want to get that kind of feedback. The former focuses on specific behavior and something that the person may not be aware they are doing. So in order to give smart feedback you need to follow the *smart principles of giving feedback*. They are:

- that your intention is to be helpful

- that if someone hasn't asked for feedback, check to be sure that they are open to it

- that it deals with specific behavior, not generalities

- that it deals with behavior that can be changed

- to describe the behavior, not evaluate it

- to describe the impact that the behavior has on you

- to accept responsibility for your own perceptions and emotion by phrasing it with an "I …"

- to check to be sure that the recipient understood your feedback in the way you intended it

- to encourage the recipient to check the feedback with other people

- that one-on-one is best unless otherwise requested

- that it is timed correctly, for example, if it's over a heated issue, don't do it "in the heat of the moment"; give everyone time to cool down and think things out.

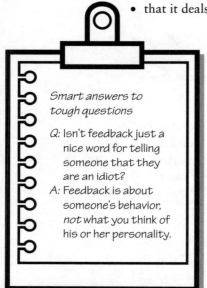

Smart answers to tough questions

Q: Isn't feedback just a nice word for telling someone that they are an idiot?
A: Feedback is about someone's behavior, *not* what you think of his or her personality.

Encouraging the recipient of feedback to check it with other people is important. It means that while you can give someone feedback, in the end it's your perception, and it would be useful for the person receiving it to check it out to see if other people see the same thing. Once you start hearing a number of people tell you the same thing, it gets harder to ignore.

Receiving feedback

Almost harder than giving feedback is receiving it. If it's positive strokes, many of us have a tendency to discount it by saying things like, "Oh it's nothing, anyone could do it." Or if it's negative to get defensive and say things like, "It's only because I didn't have enough ..."

Smart principles of receiving feedback are:

- that when you ask for feedback, be specific in describing the behavior that you want the feedback about

- try not to act defensively or rationalize

- to summarize your understanding of the feedback you've just received

- to share your thoughts and feelings about the feedback.

If you are following these principles of feedback, you shouldn't run into problems. But remember that it can be useful and necessary at times to have an objective party around to facilitate feedback! One of the interesting things I've noticed about people when they do get quality feedback is that what they are being told is usually something that they are aware of, on some level or another. Time after time when someone is given feedback on something that, for example, they should continue doing, such as asking questions and coming up with ideas for the team, they are vaguely aware that they are doing that and that it is a good thing for the team.

KILLER QUESTIONS

Do you see any value in each of us giving and receiving feedback about each other's behavior?

Part of the skill of reviewing and giving feedback is to know when you need to review and to evaluate whether the review was successful.

When most teams review, they tend to focus on tasks, procedures and business processes, failing to give attention to the team's own "processes," i.e. how the team is working together and how interpersonal dynamics are affecting the work that's being done. It probably feels "safer" and less challenging to concentrate on task issues and devote time and energy to moving these issues forward. But if your team doesn't have the ability to manage its own "processes" effectively, then you won't make much of an impact on improving the team's performance. As the smart person knows, teams are made up of tasks and relationships, and both need to be maintained.

Evaluating the effectiveness of your review is vital. You know a review has been effective when it fulfils the purpose of reviewing and:

- you can observe new behaviors

- there is an impact of greater self-awareness

- you can see learning put into action.

If you are a team that doesn't review, getting it right in terms of timing and the effectiveness of your reviews may come slowly. But get into the habit of doing it. Smart teams take the opportunity to review, whether it's formal or spur of the moment – just do it.

Reward systems

Reward systems these days have become a bit more complicated. It used to be that individuals were rewarded for their exceptional contribution. But then there is the issue of team recognition – it's not like a football team where, if you do well and hit your target, you get the World Cup or the Super Bowl.

How you are rewarded as an individual and as a team will have an effect, at least in the short term, on motivation and morale. While money may not motivate everyone, it's important to be recognized for your efforts.

Many organizations give rewards that are promotions up the corporate ladder. But that kind of promotion for an individual or team, happiest when they are coming up with creative ideas, may be taking away from them what they most enjoy, i.e., the freedom that comes with creativity and innovation.

Many companies have shied away from the matter because it seems so difficult to unravel. Smart companies base reward systems on behavior that your team and the company value and have learned to address it creatively. Letting teams choose their own rewards is gaining momentum.

Team rewards run the gamut from sharing a percentage of cost-cutting measures to calling employees' mothers to brag about them, as told by Bob Nelson in his book on energizing employees. *The smart lesson is finding out what makes a team or individual tick.*

Here are the *smart* things for you to find out about how your reward system works:

- Does your line manager/team leader have control, or is it through policy makers?

Because rewards are usually more symbolic than anything else, figuring out what makes the team tick and matching that to material reward is the key issue.

Money and rewards will hold things together for awhile, but the satisfaction from the accomplishment will last longer.

- Is the reward system tied to team performance and/or individual breadth of skills?

- In what form do we get rewarded – money, prizes, praise?

- What happens if your project doesn't have a measurable monetary value attached to it, like improving customer service; who will find the objective measuring stick, and how?

For many organizations it seems impossible not to recognize the individual. But be sure that it doesn't set-up competition and a pecking order within the team. *Also be sure that you have an attainable target to aim for,* otherwise you won't feel as though you are being taken seriously.

Organizations are also starting to use rewards to create some competition between internal teams. You can see the obvious advantage for the organization, they'll get people working harder and faster. But be aware that it can create sour grapes as well.

SMART VOICES

At a large brewery, the first construction team to complete building a new site in 20 weeks would win a week away. However, after the first team completed, and won, the others claimed that they had the "right" and "easier" site to work on.

Smart things
to say about
teams

And you also don't want to feel that the reward is so easy to get that you really don't need to deliver anything. If you expect it, then it isn't anything special.

Teams as well as individuals need to recognize their achievements and celebrate their success. So while you may be rewarded by the organization, don't forget to celebrate success within the team. But just like rewards, it needs to come from a sincere appreciation of the work that has been done. Giving yourself a pat on the back every time you dot the i or cross the t can be pretty obnoxious and boring.

This chapter has given you a chance to take a look at what it takes to get results from a team. Although having a goal is important, setting SMART goals is the only way forward. We've looked at problem-solving and how creative thinking and/or lateral thinking also helps to get results.

But knowing whether you really are "making it so" requires the hard work and time out to have team reviews. And within those reviews must be the maturity and ability of team members to give and receive quality feedback. And I haven't forgotten that you need to understand what to look for when you want to reward a team.

7

Help is on the Way

TOOLS AND TECHNIQUES YOU MAY ENCOUNTER

Let him that would move the world, first move himself.

Socrates

Understanding how teams and people operate will help you to be successful in your team and for the team to be successful. There are a lot of different "tools" out there to help you get that understanding. But the first step in understanding what makes other people tick, is for you to understand how you do. This chapter discusses a few of the most common tools, techniques, and training that you may come across. You may feel that some of them are just labels or ways of putting yourself or others into a box, but the idea behind creating these "labels" is that it gives you a different way of looking at things. Often a way of understanding differences between yourself and others.

> One of the underlying assumptions made about people working together is that everyone is appreciated for what they bring to the team. Unfortunately relationships don't always pan out that way. A difference in working styles has stymied many a relationship.

Most of the tools that are discussed in this chapter are things that someone else has decided would be beneficial to you and your team. You may or may not have any control over whether you participate or not. It is not a death sentence; it doesn't mean you will be staring down the barrel of truth, baring your soul to those around you. It does mean that you will have the opportunity to learn something about yourself, your style of working and your preferred approach, as well as those around you.

The way we are

Understanding yourself and others

Most of the tools you will encounter will give you information about yourself. Whether it's learning styles, how you interpret information, or what kind of potential you may have as a "leader," the focus is placed on raising an awareness of yourself. Getting this kind of information can be incredibly useful and fun to learn. But, I must add a caveat here: *it's only useful when you use them as a tool for understanding and never as an excuse for how you behave.* No one learns or develops from the statement, "that's just the way I am." While that may be true, you are ultimately held responsible for who you are, and the actions and behaviors that make you "the way you are."

So while you will learn about yourself, you can make the information relevant to the team if you share it. But remember that not everyone may

A[n] ... important point about training events takes us back to the issue of responsibility, not only for learning itself, but with applying it in the workplace ... A [training] event which looks at developing awareness or interpersonal skills ... [is] unlikely to be able ... in a short space of time, to fundamentally change people's behavior. The responsibility for transferring understanding into long-term changes in the way we behave back at work remains with the individual concerned and must be supported through actions taken in the workplace.

Derek Furze and Chris Gale, *Interpreting Management*

be open to the idea of sharing. If they are, you have a great opportunity to learn and understand why team members behave in certain ways. So for example, instead of thinking it's because of who I am that Sharon and I have a problem, maybe it's because your "styles and perceptions" are just very different.

Don't let your past get in your way. Be careful not to be reminded of someone else and therefore interact with them based on your old relationship. Give them the chance to be themselves. All too often we treat people based on some perception we have of who they might be, because they remind us of someone else. That could be a big mistake, especially if they are better intentioned than the person they remind you of.

Smart quotes

The illiterate of the 21st century will not be those who cannot read and write, but those who cannot learn, unlearn and relearn.

Alvin Toffler

In the end, getting help means getting new information and input, it also means learning, about yourself and possibly others. Key to success in this area is open-mindedness. So, let's start by looking at how we learn.

Learning-style inventory

Learning is important not only because it increases your capabilities, but also your learning style influences how you approach work, how you contribute to the team, and sometimes how easily you may fit in with a team. David Kolb developed the cycle of experiential learning. Kolb thinks we can use experience to learn through the following continuous cycle:

- *do* – as in a task or job – have a concrete experience

- *review* – draw out key learning through observation and reflection

- *modify* – form concepts and ideas for improvement

- *apply* – test implications of concepts in a new situation.

This learning process is meant to be continuously recurring. We test our concepts in experience and modify them as a result of our observations of the experience. Experiential learning, as this is called, is how most of us learn as adults. We have an experience and then learn from that experience. Some of us instinctively stop to review what has happened, others modify it – forming concepts and ideas for improvement, but we then store what we've "learned" from the experience into our memories to be applied at a later date to a new situation.

Smart things to say about teams

Success in the marketplace increasingly depends on learning, yet most people don't know how to learn. What's more, those members of the organization that many assume to be the best at learning are, in fact, not very good at it.

Chris Argyris

Kolb says that your needs and goals govern the direction of learning, that this experiential learning process is focused around goals. So if your goals and needs are not clear, then the process of learning will be inefficient and erratic.

If your learning is based on your goals, then learning becomes very individual. So for example, the scientist guy in the team may be interested in forming concepts and ideas for improvement, but the marketing manager will be more interested in the concrete experiences, the sales of the product.

Kolb said that most people are naturally drawn to one or two phases of the experiential learning cycle. He labelled them as:

- *divergent thinkers* – the people who are good at identifying problems – they are the brainstormers because they can see things from different perspectives

- *assimilators* – they are the people who make the connections, they draw hypotheses and suggest reasons why something happened, they are the "system thinkers"

- *convergent thinkers* – the solution finders, they are good at abstraction, but also experimentation

- *accommodators* – their strength lies in doing things, in moving the assimilators on to carrying out the plans.

Kolb suggests that the most powerful teams have representatives from all four cycles. *To be an effective team you need to provide time for both action (doing and applying) and reflection (reviewing and modifying).*

If you now apply this cycle to problem-solving – you can begin to see how different people with different styles can help you to get through a problem, starting with the brainstormers. You just need to get the right people in the right place at the right time.

From this work, Kolb copyrighted the diagnostic tool *Learning Style Inventory (LSI)*. It was developed to help individuals identify their learning styles. A very similar tool to help you discover your team's learning style is the *Learning Style Diagnostic Questionnaire (LSDQ)* developed by Peter Honey and Alan Mumford.

Why are learning styles important to a team? Learning increases your capabilities and capacity, and a team can potentially improve it's capability, either by bringing in someone who is good at doing what the team lacks, or by developing the skills from within the team.

SMART PEOPLE
TO HAVE ON
YOUR SIDE:

ROYAL DUTCH
SHELL

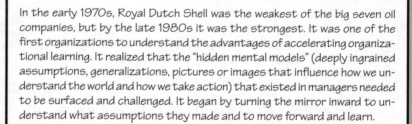

In the early 1970s, Royal Dutch Shell was the weakest of the big seven oil companies, but by the late 1980s it was the strongest. It was one of the first organizations to understand the advantages of accelerating organizational learning. It realized that the "hidden mental models" (deeply ingrained assumptions, generalizations, pictures or images that influence how we understand the world and how we take action) that existed in managers needed to be surfaced and challenged. It began by turning the mirror inward to understand what assumptions they made and to move forward and learn.

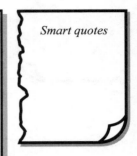

Smart quotes

If you happen to be the "leader" of a team, you can see how your predominant style may dangerously influence what you place importance on. Charles Handy, management theorist and author, suggests that the key role of the leader is to "keep the wheel moving." That means getting those right people in the right place, knowing when it's time to move on from brainstorming and to make some connections.

Myers Briggs Type Indicator

The Myers Briggs Type Indicator (MBTI) has been around either in theory or practice, since the 1920s. Many books have been written about it, from the guidebook covering the history and statistical analysis, to the newsletter published by the Association of Psychological Type (yes there is one). One of the reasons it gets so much airtime and analysis is because of the in-depth, accurate and entertaining conclusions it can provide.

Katherine Briggs and Isabel Briggs Myers (the mother and daughter that developed the questionnaire) believed that human behavior is not random but predictable, and that the differences are the result of our preferences. A simple idea, based on the psychiatrist C.G. Jung's work.

Organizations use MBTI to help to determine what those individual differences are, so that instead of name-calling as we know it, you can start "name-calling" with skill. A great thing about MBTI is that it can help you to communicate more effectively – if you can understand each other's differences, you can begin to see eye to eye, you'll then work more effectively.

Myers and Briggs argue that we all have different ways of doing the following and the different "types" that describe them. They are:

Smart quotes

That is what learning is. You suddenly understand something you've understood all your life, but in a new way.

Doris Lessing (novelist)

Where you get your energy

- *Extrovert* – you get your energy from the outside world, love to be in touch with people, and for example after a bad day in the office would call a good friend or meet them for a drink to bring your energy back, you need to verbalize what is happening. Very often known to speak before you think.

- *Introvert* – you get your energy from internal sources, find being interrupted very disruptive and for example, would rather take a hot bath and read a book to bring your energy levels back up, you prefer to keep your observations and decisions inside. Very often known to think before you speak.

How you take in information

- *Sensing* – you see the parts instead of the whole. So if there were glasses, beer and a bag of potato chips on the table, you would see them as individual items. You are quite literal about taking in information, interested in the here and now.

- *Intuitive* – you see the whole picture and then the parts. So if you had the glasses, beer and bag of potato chips, you would look at it and say "Party!" You are figurative about taking in information and look for possibilities and meanings.

How you make decisions

- *Thinking* – you prefer to make decisions objectively based on logic and analysis. You are looking for justice and clarity and tend not to get personally involved in a decision. You make decisions with your "head."

- *Feeling* – you prefer to make decisions driven by an interpersonal involvement. You are looking for harmony, the impact of the decision on people is extremely important to you. You make decisions with your "heart."

How you orient your life

- *Judgment* – you prefer to have life organized. It's structured and scheduled, ordered, planned and controlled. You usually feel there is a right way and a wrong way of doing things. You often get frustrated by people being late.

- *Perceiving* – you prefer to let life just happen. It's flexible, spontaneous, adaptive and responsive. You have a wait-and-see attitude about most things. Often known to say, "what deadline?"

Katharine Briggs started getting interested in classifying people based on their differences in living styles back at the turn of the 20th century. She developed her work even before she stumbled across the psychiatrist C.G. Jung's work. Once she discovered his work in the 1920s, she dedicated herself to the study of Jung. What makes both Jung and Briggs unusual is at the time that they started making the distinction that, as Briggs put it, different people approach life differently, they were running counter to what the rest of the psychiatry world believed. They were talking about preferences instead of sicknesses or abnormalities.

Katharine had a daughter, Isabel Briggs Myers, who helped her develop the questionnaire throughout the 1930s by "type watching" people. They started with their friends and family and spent the next twenty years gathering a phenomenal amount of data on different populations. Katharine also developed a fourth scale to Jung's work, which became the Judgement/Perception scale. The onslaught of World War II, and their observation that many people in the war effort were working in tasks unsuited to their abilities, set them on their way to design the psychological instrument called the Myers Briggs Type Indicator. These two women were incredibly smart, dedicated and driven, they were self-taught not only in psychology, but in statistics as well. Once the MBTI instrument was developed, Isabel learned and ran statistical analysis on the data collected to prove the validity of the instrument.

MBTI is now one of the most widely used psychological instruments worldwide and has been translated into at least five languages.

Taking MBTI means completing a questionnaire, the "results" will be your type, which is a four-letter combination. This will give you an indication as to where your preferences lie. It takes a while to get used to the "Myers Briggs" speak, but stick it out, it's useful.

Getting the best of MBTI

To get the best out of the MBTI is to just take it. And that means not thinking too long about each of the questions, but just getting on with it. I remember taking it and thinking, these are such stupid and annoying questions, I can't believe that this will be of any use to me. What are some of the *smart* things you need to know about it?

- There is no "right type." MBTI gives you results about your tendencies and preferences, it doesn't reflect your intelligence levels or likelihood of success.

- Just because you come out with a preference in one area, doesn't mean you don't possess characteristics from the opposite end of the scale. For example, if you are a thinking type it doesn't mean you don't use your feelings as part of your decision-making process. You just prefer to use your thinking.

- While all of it will be true, not all of it is the truth. There are 16 types, imagine if the whole population was given the questionnaire, everyone would fit into the 16 types. That gives an awful lot of scope for different kinds of people within each type. While it is very useful, it won't tell you everything you need to know about yourself and others. As human beings we are, fortunately, more complicated than that.

The usual way of looking at groups and leadership, as separate phenomena, is no longer adequate. The most exciting groups ... those that shook the world – resulted from a mutually respectful marriage between an able leader and an assemblage of extraordinary people. Groups become great only when everyone in them, leaders and members alike, is free to do his or her absolute best.

Warren Bennis, *Organizing Genius; The Secrets of Creative Collaboration*

- You may have an inclination to game it, but because the information is useful to you as an individual and as you work in a team, don't try and second-guess it.

- Is it possible to second-guess it? Possibly – but for what purpose? If it's being used during a job-placement interview, it won't get you anywhere because you'll just have to be yourself once you get the job.

- As for the interviewing process, it gives the employer an indication of how you may perceive the world and your style of working, it doesn't tell them what kind of employee you may turn out to be.

What happens if you get your MBTI type and you don't agree with all of it? There's always that possibility – you know yourself better than a questionnaire does. But that doesn't mean that the tool is useless. If you find yourself there, it's really useful to talk about it, especially with people who know you well and ask them what they think. For example, a woman on a course came out as an ISTP, but felt that the T (Thinking dimension) was not right, that she was more a Feeling type. It wasn't until she went home and talked to her husband about how they made decisions, he was an ESFP, that she realized she definitely was a Thinking type.

> **Smart things to say about teams**
>
> Sometimes you need to look at how your "type" behaves under stress in order to determine whether you agree with the questionnaire results.

How to make MBTI work for you

The hardest part about MBTI is not just taking it and getting the information about yourself, but understanding how to apply it. It's a real "what now?" Here are some questions you can use with others that will get you to start applying MBTI:

- In type terms, where are we the same?

- Where are we different?

- Where might we have trouble communicating in terms of our types – for example, if you are two Intuitive types, you could each have an idea/concept that you are convinced is the "right one."

- Where do you actually have trouble communicating – how does the answer to the previous question reflect reality?

- How could your type differences be a positive factor?

It is also useful for you to start looking at your own type bias and start to notice how you communicate because of it. For example, if you are an Extrovert, you are probably inclined to think as you talk, not noticing that you're answering your own questions before anyone else has a chance to. Maybe that's because many of the people around you are Introverts, and Introverts, generally, need to think about things first before they speak. They don't have the chance to get a word in edgewise before you move on to the next issue.

KILLER QUESTIONS

In what way would MBTI be useful for this team?

Another example of making MBTI work for you is when you have to make a presentation. If you become more aware of your own "type" you can then try and adapt the presentation to be sure that you are addressing other types' needs. For example, the Intuitive who gives a marketing presentation that talks primarily about possibilities will need to include the practicalities of their ideas for the Sensing types.

You know that accepting other people's differences is easier said than done. A laid-back approach for one person, could just be plain old lazy to another. MBTI can help you to get a quicker understanding of what might be going on and why you may be butting heads with someone.

Jane and Paul, consultants, were working on restructuring a department at an external client. They started to run into trouble when it came time to make decisions about how to restructure individual roles. Jane looked at how the changes would impact the individuals and the relationships, and wanted to ensure that while the changes would be hard, people's feelings were also being taken into account. Paul, on the other hand, didn't see the point. He thought that people's feelings about the changes were solely the client's responsibility. He and Jane had more important business issues to deal with than to think about what everyone was feeling. After the first few days of working together, Jane and Paul luckily realized that they couldn't continue to work this way, especially since their internal meetings continued to be more and more heated. After a number of unsuccessful attempts to discuss their differences rationally, they stopped to look at their Myers Briggs types and found that their differences lay in their decision-making preference. Jane made decisions using her Feeling dimension, Paul with his Thinking. Once they realized this, and knew that both were important, they found it easier not only to work together, but also to see the situation from the other's point of view.

Relationships are complicated, and you can't always rely on MBTI to give you the answers, but it can certainly help you start looking in other places than saying – "hey, it's his/her problem not mine."

Once you learn about your preferences, watch out: our strengths can lead to our weaknesses. Take for example someone whose natural style is to generate ideas and inspire big-picture thinking. Many organizations value this kind of thinking and you may find yourself being promoted, possibly heading your own division or own company. These positions call for a lot of discipline and attention to details, which idea generators find stressful and uninteresting. If you don't identify this as being a problem and delegate or find another way of coping with it, then you could burnout very quickly. Your strength could lead to a weakness.

There are not dependent people and dominant people. There are not autonomous people and participative people. This is the psychologist's viewpoint, who then wants to create a personality test to identify empowered employees and empowering managers and use the results to select and develop the right people. Viewing the solution as a talent search so externalizes the problem that we stay immobile, stuck on that wooden horse where we began.

Instead, hold on to the idea that there is a dependent and autonomous part of each of us. There is also a dominant and yielding part of each of us. Accepting this thought does two things. First it places the problem within our control, rather than projecting it onto others. To speak as if we are empowered and those people are not, as if we have claimed our freedom and they have not, is just a subtle form of some Darwinian wish to be further along than others. By acknowledging the struggle as ours, we keep ourselves humble and focussed on the right spot. Second, it means there is hope for those who seem to resist the ideas of partnership and empowerment and the responsibility that goes along with them. If there is in each person a wish for more autonomy and a wish to give up control, then it gives us something in each person to speak to.

Peter Block, *Stewardship, Choosing Service over Self-Interest*

Who prefers MBTI?

Because of the nature of MBTI, it's about possibilities and relationships between and among people, you will find that Intuitives will be the "type" most interested in it. Intuitives like to think and talk about possibilities and MBTI feeds that interest.

This doesn't mean that Sensing types will not be interested in MBTI or any less adept at using it. You may just find that Sensing types don't find it as "fascinating" or useful as Intuitives do.

A group of management consultants were having a training session on MBTI. Within the group there were eight Intuitive and three Sensing types. The trainer decided to set up an exercise, which separated the two types and asked them to come up with a list of questions they would like to ask each other – what would be important for them to know about the other type.

The results were hilarious. The Intuitives sat around talking about why they thought it would be important to get this kind of information from the other group. In the end they barely came up with a relevant question for the Sensing group. In the mean time the Sensing group came in and said "we're only interested in one question – how do Intuitives make your type look so sexy? Other than that we're not really interested in what the possibilities are."

Both groups acted exactly as their type would expect them. The Intuitives looked for theory and the concepts behind it all. And the Sensing types just wanted to know the facts.

How about those teams?

Recognizing differences between people in teams and accepting them can make your day a whole lot easier. That's pretty easy to say, but the next time so and so is late for a meeting, as usual, which camp will you fall into? The "I'll get you for being late" camp where anything that the late-comer says is shot down; or do you talk about how much it annoys you?

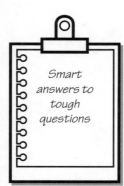

Smart answers to tough questions

Q: Isn't MBTI just another management trick and fad to force us to accept more crap, i.e. less people doing more work?

A: It's difficult to believe that management will get anything sinister from using MBTI – the tool was developed to provide information for the individual. OK, so your company may get something out of it if you are going to resolve some differences with colleagues, but hey, they're paying for it.

You then come to an agreement that in the future meetings will start on time – full attendance or not.

In their book *Type Talk* Otto Krueger and Janet Thuesen offer some useful suggestions for creating an effective team:

- *Are the types represented on the team the best ones to get the job done?* Not all teams require every preference. Some types of goals are achieved more quickly or efficiently by teams that are more alike than different.

Whole Foods is the largest natural-foods grocer in the United States. They believe that all work is teamwork, they have an open policy where everyone sees the financial numbers, executives have a salary cap of no more than eight times the average wage, and people vote on who gets hired. The culture is left over from when it was a corner health-food store.

The culture is premised on decentralized teamwork, which means that the team, not the hierarchy is the defining unit of activity. Each of the stores is an autonomous profit center made up of an average of 10 self-managed teams. Team leaders in each store are a team; store leaders in each region are a team; and the company's regional presidents are a team.

They are a high-trust organization not only because the whole team decides (two-thirds vote) who gets hired, but because of their open-salary policy. Every store has a book that lists the previous year's salary and bonuses for all the employees in the organization.

Employees all have access to the company's financial and operation data. John Mackey, CEO calls it a "no-secrets" management philosophy. In most companies where management controls the information, they therefore control the people. They believe that with an open policy they stay "aligned to the vision of shared fate." He says that "if you are trying to create a high-trust organization, where people are all-for-one and one-for-all, you can't have secrets."

SMART PEOPLE
TO HAVE ON
YOUR SIDE:

WHOLE FOODS
MARKETS INC.

If you are trying to come up with some ideas in a brainstorming session, the more Extroverts and Intuitives the better.

- *Within the team, are the right types doing the right jobs?* Many times we have skills that are untapped, either because we are out of the habit or because people don't declare them. They just need to be recognized, so a team assessment of skills would be useful.

- *How will we check our progress along the way?* A mix of types will help here, the Judgers to keep on course, but Perceivers to ensure that the team doesn't make good time going in the wrong direction. Also Introverts will keep you listening and Feelers will make sure that people's ideas aren't wrongly dismissed.

- *Is there someone who can help determine when the job is done?* If a team's reached its goal, it can be pretty hard to let go – success or failure. You need someone who's going to speak up and tell the group to get on with it. Usually an Extrovert and some Judgers.

While this advice has been put into a MBTI context, I think that they are incredibly useful questions to ask the team, even if you're not into MBTI.

MBTI is complicated and takes a while to digest. If you are going to have it "done" to your team you need to ask some questions …

KILLER
QUESTIONS

- Will we be expected to keep MBTI "alive" on our own or will we have more support to further understand it?
- How will it be reinforced in everyday work situations?
- How many other teams/departments will be using it?
- Is it being used to "assess" our team?
- Who else will know our preference types?
- What does it say about our team as a whole?

Specifically for teams

While identifying team roles starts with identifying individual roles, some diagnostic tools were specifically designed with teams in mind.

Belbin team roles

Meredith Belbin is a British academic who pioneered work in the late 1960s. Belbin was interested in team performance and how it might be influenced by the kinds of people making up a team.

Belbin came up with two important conclusions:

- Teams composed of the brightest and most accomplished managers did not perform anywhere near the best. They had too many cooks for the soup pot.

- The most effective teams, especially during lots of change, require nine different roles.

The roles that Belbin refers to are not your typical manager, assistant, marketing type roles; they are much less formal. These roles relate to your personality, skills and attributes (not that job titles don't) but they are often more influential than the "formal" ones. Belbin believed that if you developed an understanding of the contributions you make to a team, you could create a more effective team. The nine archetypal roles go like this:

- *Plant* – the creative, imaginative and unorthodox person. You solve difficult problems. So if you are in a burning building, you will be trying to figure out how to get out. Problem is you'll come up with lots of best routes out – but won't make a decision about which one should be taken.

- *Shaper* – the dynamic, outgoing, highly strung individual in the team. You like to challenge and pressurize as well as find ways around obstacles. You'll take one of the plant's ideas and get everyone going.

- *Co-ordinator* – the calm, confident and trusting individual. You welcome all potential contributors on their merits and keep prejudice out of the way as well as being objective. You make sure that everyone else's ideas about how to get out of the burning building are heard as well as the plant's.

- *Implementer* – the disciplined, reliable, conservative and efficient individual. You are great at organizing, have lots of common sense and are hard-working. But once you get your mind set on which way out of the burning building is best, it may be difficult to change it.

- *Teamworker* – the supportive, popular and collaborative individual. You are very people-oriented, listen, build relationships, but probably avoid friction. Your focus is on team relationships and you like co-operation.

- *Resource investigator* – the extrovert, who is enthusiastic, a communicator, and likes to explore opportunities. The ultimate networker. You're great at using contacts and ideas from outside the team.

- *Specialist* – single-minded individual that is self-starting and dedicated. You will have a great deal of knowledge about very specific things, but very little knowledge on lots of things.

- *Monitor evaluator* – strategic, discerning and sober. You see all the options and make judgements. Team members know that when they come to you with a question, you will have spent a great deal of time thinking all the options through.

- *Completer* – conscientious, anxious and delivers on time. You're the one who dots the "i"s and crosses the "t"s.

We all have the capacity to operate in each of these roles, but Belbin believes that you will have a strong preference for one or two roles and will operate more effectively in that way. In reality, the chances are that individuals will step up to bat filling the roles necessary depending upon the work and the circumstances. For example, you may come out with strong preferences as a resources investigator and a shaper, but that doesn't mean you wouldn't be imaginative and creative, filling the plant role, if the need arises.

Each role can make important contributions to a team, and if you look at the balance of the team and see where there may be some "weaknesses," you can determine who can slot into these roles. You won't be an effective

There is a danger that once someone decides that they are a "completer" for example, they may assume they have no creative or coordinating abilities. This can easily lead to stereotyping themselves (or others), restricting the potential of both the individual and the team.

Derek Furze and Chris Gale, *Interpreting Management*

team if no-one keeps the momentum going and pushes through obstacles (shaper) or finishes off the work and checks all the details (completer).

Belbin's roles are particularly good at highlighting the differences among members of a team, and to start to get people to see how someone else's "annoying" habits, are actually very useful for the team to get things done. On the other hand, be careful not to get too stuck on a label, you don't want to get too boxed in.

Belbin is good fun, and lots of people look at the results and say – "I can't believe how accurate this is, that really is me." Well of course it is, it's a self-assessment – you answered the questions. But aside from the obvious, it does come up with some good descriptions and can give you a handle on what you may excel at. And as has already been said, it's especially useful for team members in helping to understand each other.

Belbin's work has been criticized in the past, particularly by professionals working in the trade because it has no statistical analysis behind it, but it has proved quite useful for us everyday folk.

Like all of these "psychometric tools" they are fun because they give you an opportunity to talk about yourself, and to get some feedback about the way that you work. They are often used in team development courses, because they take the "issues" out of context, which makes talking and seeing things in a non-judgmental and non-personal light.

Team development courses

You could find yourself on a team development or team building course for a variety of reasons. It could be that you need to work through problems with your current project, you're a new team needing to establish working practices, or because there are "people problems." Whatever the case may be, it gives everyone the opportunity to do some navel gazing. These courses usually take place away from the office and the locations run the gamut from luxurious five-star hotels to a night or two up a mountain in a tent. But don't feel gypped if you find that your course is being run at home base – it could be that your only other choice was two days in a tent in the rain.

If you are going on a course where there are not specific technical skills being taught, what you should have is a facilitator, either from within the organization or an outside consultant. They probably won't be someone who has something to "teach" you because they know the answers. Most teams have the answers within them already, it's just a question of tapping into it, and getting people to see things a bit differently – that's what a good facilitator will do. They get your team to see things from a different point of view or from each other's.

Being on a course like this can be a bit confusing, it's not like an IT course, where you walk away with skills and are able to use them right away. What you will learn from them will be much less tangible. While the course may be designed to unlock some of the work-related issues that exist, it may also help you to understand how the team interacts. If it's geared up for the latter, then the smart person will learn and understand what kinds of behaviors are working for and against you and the team.

There are a number of issues that can be addressed in these kinds of courses:

- looking at stresses within and outside the team

- identifying and building on strengths of the team

- examining and building levels of co-operation

- looking at decision-making processes used within the team

- creating vision and direction for the team

- clarifying goals and objectives

- recognizing strengths and differences of individuals

- developing your interpersonal skills.

This is by no means a complete list of issues, but it will start to give you an understanding of where they can go. These courses should be designed to develop skills that already exist but you may not be aware of; like muscles, you know they are there, but they need to be strengthened. You will spend time putting your team under the microscope, and at times may feel as if you are splitting hairs.

We know that personal skills and management training for individuals has little impact on changing organizations. It becomes difficult for an individual to sustain new behaviors in an old environment. Yet we still send individuals to training programs. If our intent is to create community, and teams are a vehicle for doing that, we should offer training that is attended primarily by teams. No team, no training … Technical training may be an exception, but when we offer training for people one at a time, we are supporting individualism and missing an opportunity.

Peter Block, *Stewardship, Choosing Service over Self-Interest*

A well-designed course will have gathered information before the course, preferably, but not always, from your whole team to discuss what the issues are. The person designing the course will have a better chance of getting it right, if they have some first hand experience with the team.

While indoor and outdoor courses very often try to address the same issues, their methodology can sometimes be very different. At least the experience will be. Now don't get me wrong, there are thousands of different courses that have been developed, and there are just as many different methods of developing people or as some call it "unleashing potential." Types of development course seem to go in and out of fashion as quickly as management jargon does. The Western world seems to have taken many an Eastern philosophy under its wing as well, and while each will have different attributes, one cannot say which one will really work for you. It usually comes down to style.

**KILLER
QUESTIONS**

- What kind of pre-course work will there be – will we meet with the facilitator/trainer first to discuss issues and set the objectives of the course?
- What style of delivery can we expect – lecture or discussion-based?
- If exercises or tasks are involved, is there just as much or more time for facilitated team reviews and discussions, i.e., learning to take place?
- Will there be pressure to participate in any physical activity (e.g., climbing, abseiling, meditation)?
- What kind of follow-up will there be back at work?
- How will a transfer of learning be supported back at work?

Outdoor courses

Team-building courses that happen in the outdoors are still popular; they tend to leave work back at the office, and try to re-create the dynamics of the team by giving you a series of exercises, designed to address different topics (experiential learning). The philosophy is that the way you interact doing these exercises will be similar to the way that you interact back at the office. Especially important to these types of course is that enough time has been factored into the program to allow for facilitated reviews. If you are

SMART VOICES

I think that disruption in teams is often not related to the project, but to the way people deal with each other (i.e. not listening or being "wound up" by types they find difficult). Talking and being honest often resolves this, especially if the team is going through a crisis. What I came across was "undercurrents" of bad feeling and simmering resentment. So when we had a day out of the office with a facilitator, I was very honest about my feelings about the team and this seemed to encourage others to do likewise. It was useful to stop focusing on what we do and concentrate on how we do it – how the group worked together.

Rhona Richard (Production Manager, Blackwell Publishers)

going from exercise to exercise – this is not a development course, you may have a good time, and learn something about each other, but that will be a side effect. A development course on the other hand must have separate time allocated for discussion which should be run by a trained facilitator.

It's worth talking about the fear issues concerning out-door courses. Lots of people think of the military type course that wakes you up in the middle of the night and sends you out into the cold. While some of them still exist (and seem to be coming back into popularity) for the most part it's changed. Physical challenge and sleep deprivation are *not* what a course should be about. A good outdoor course will at some point, but not throughout, give individuals the opportunity to stretch themselves physically if they like, with support from team members. However, the prime aim is not physically to challenge and over-stretch an individual to the point of panic. You won't learn anything, except maybe how scared you are of say, abseiling. At no point should anyone feel unsafe or pressured to do something physically they are not comfortable with.

> *Smart things to say about teams*
>
> The idea is to stretch yourself beyond what would feel comfortable, but not so far that you feel like panicking.

Another criticism of outdoor courses is that it can be difficult to translate some of the learning back to the office. Because you have been doing exercises that are unrelated to the work-place it may feel out of context. It's all well and good to learn something from an exercise that no-one has any great interest in other than completing, but the chances are your work isn't that cut and dried.

Professor Reginald Revans is scathing about the value of traditional "chalk and talk" management education which prevailed during the 1960s and 1970s. He argues that people learn most effectively not from books, lecturers or teachers, but from sharing real problems with others.

SMART VOICES

So why bother working in the outdoors? Well, for one they break down hierarchy barriers. For example, the more senior members of the group will not necessarily have a higher level of expertise in a different environment. Also because the outcome of the exercises and tasks you are given on an outdoor course doesn't affect your team back at the office, you are less at risk and may find talking about what's happening within the group during reviews a bit easier. They can also be a good laugh, as well as a great way to get to know each other better. Some teams that struggle with developing a social side find that outdoor courses can help to build the relationships within the team. There's nothing like everyone being in the same situation away from work, in the sunshine, slogging it up a hill together.

But how do you make it work back at work? The following holds true for any kind of course – indoors or outdoors:

- keep asking the question, how will we make this work back at the office, while you're on the course

- be sure there's time for action-planning at the end of the course – and most importantly that individuals are allocated responsibility for making it happen back at work

- chase up the people who organized it in the first place to give you some support.

Time after time, teams go on courses, decide to change something, but find that once they get back, their work environment it isn't geared up for change. Don't let it stop you, getting the resources for change is vital and the kind of support that teams need – appeal to the "powers that be" for support.

The cross-functional team of an industrial equipment manufacturer which consisted of sales, customer reps (the people who took over after the salesmen) and engineering, and were spread across Europe and Asia went on an outdoor team development course. The team was in the business of producing a made-to-order machine for their clients that was difficult to manage from the initial sales call to final production. There tended to be a lot of finger pointing from engineering to customer reps and from customer reps to salesmen if there were any specification problems in production. The salesmen traveled extensively and it was difficult for the customer reps to be in contact with them, so the hand-over of information in their early meetings was very important. By the end of the course they realized that the salesmen had a lot of information that would be very useful, even though they had "fallen out of the loop." Part of the action plan they developed was to have meetings more regularly between the three functions. Because they were based in different parts of the world, they found that real-time meetings weren't always possible. No problem – they'd videoconference on a monthly basis. Once they got back to their offices they found only one of the three offices was geared up for videoconferencing. Getting it to happen was by far the hardest thing they had to do on return. The key success factor was that two of the customer reps took responsibility for seeing it through and kept the ball rolling.

Simpson Desert

In the late 1950s during the Humanistic Movement, NASA was looking at putting teams together to travel into space. They realized that people needed more than academic and physical problem solving abilities to operate effectively as part of a group. They came up with an exercise, Survival on the Moon, which looked at and assessed how people operate in teams. Simpson Desert is based on these same principles. The key to these exercises is to look at and assess individual and group decision-making. And the way that they work is as follows.

Q: If we aren't learning any technical skills on a course, what good will it do for us?

A: Experiential learning courses are designed to help you understand the processes the team may use for things like decision-making, levels of participation and influencing.

People in a team are given a problem – how to survive in the desert/on the moon/or other variations on the theme. You are then given a list of items that you have available for survival. As an individual you need to rank in order of importance what you would need to survive. You then go back into the team and come up with a team ranking, without using a voting system to help your team come up with a decision.

The purpose of the exercise is not to get the same ranking as the experts who could "survive on the moon," but to:

• look at the process of how the team reached their decisions

• look at how people get their own ideas across in a group, or not.

It doesn't matter if you've done this exercise (indeed many of the exercises you may come across) before or not. "Knowing the answer" isn't what's important, it's how the team got to their answer that is important. Also if you've done the exercise before, your behavior in this team is likely to be different from how you are in others.

Time after time in this exercise, the team ranking is 70% closer to that of the "expert" (which means survival) than any individual's ranking. But the team ranking is only better when the sum of the team is better than any one individual. For example, if you have someone who has survived in the desert or on the moon, then he/she could probably be considered an "expert" in the team and his/her ranking *may* come closer on its own than the team's.

For example, a buying team for a womenswear company were on a course doing the Simpson Desert exercise. One of the team members started off the team decision-making session by saying, "OK, I've done a desert survival course, I think that I have a good idea of what the ranking should be." The team went on to ignore his experience and developed their own ranking. The team wouldn't have survived, but on his own he would have.

Another key issue about this exercise is that if the fundamental premise of the team is wrong, i.e., we can survive for 72 hours without help, then everything is wrong. So not only does it get the team to look at its decision-making process, but also how and why it makes assumptions.

This chapter has given you the opportunity to look at some of the most common tools, techniques and training that you may encounter including:

- Learning Style Inventory (LSI)

- Myers Briggs Type Indicator (MBTI)

- Belbin Team Roles

- Team development courses

- Simpson Desert.

LSI is important to a team because learning increases a team's capabilities. If you are aware of individual team members' learning styles, you have the

Smart quotes

The person who figures out how to harness the collective genius of the people in his or her organization is going to blow the competition away.

Walter Wriston (banker)

potential to increase the team's capabilities by either bringing in someone who is good at doing what the team lacks or by developing from within.

MBTI helps to identify and characterize the styles of interaction that you may use. It looks at how we interact with others and what our preferred styles may be. It is useful for teams because it can enhance your knowledge and understanding of team members, which is key to building and maintaining good relationships.

Belbin's Team Roles help you to identify what roles exist within the team and how, as Belbin would say, to develop the most effective team by filling all nine roles. This may come from the individuals already within the team or from the outside, but it gives you a chance to identify what may be necessary to make the team tick more effectively.

Team development courses are usually put together because they are trying to identify and/or develop a strength or weakness within the team. They don't teach technical skills, but instead focus on interpersonal skills or issues that the team may be facing, for example, how to communicate more effectively.

Simpson Desert is an exercise that is commonly used to get teams to look the process they use to reach decisions and how people get their ideas across in a group. It's a good opportunity for your team to get a solid view on these processes.

You've now got a good handle on how to get the best of these and to understand how they can be useful and great helpers.

8
Out There

How come when I want a pair of hands I get a human being as well?

Henry Ford

This chapter looks at four different organizations. Three of these organizations rely heavily on a team approach and we look at how they make teams work for them. The fourth relies on a co-operative structure throughout the whole organization. They all stand out, because they believe that their employees matter and how they behave towards them is important, and that includes what kinds of framework they must work within. This isn't to say they don't have obstacles to overcome, but each is striving to be more successful not just by focussing on getting more business by being better at marketing, sales or strategy, but by focussing on how things work on the inside, within the organization. But you be the judge.

At the end of each "story" is a section called *Now What?* It gives you some suggestions, ideas, and questions based on some of the practices from these organizations to try out in your team/organization.

E-Lab, LLC

E-Lab believes in teams. So much so that the whole organization's structure is based around teams and the model of practice communities (expertise lies within these communities). E-Lab is in the business of helping its clients to understand their customers better. E-Lab analyzes behavior by looking at what customers and employees do and why they do it. They then make recommendations to their clients to help identify opportunities that might otherwise have been overlooked. The approach is a broad and systematic integration of research and design.

E-Lab has found that the best way to find solutions for clients is through teams. In fact, its offices both physically and organizationally are set up to support and develop this.

The company comprises of three "practices" – Research, Design and Business, which is where their expertise lies and in effect how it "categorizes" staff. Each of these three practices has a director who in turn has a small staff designed for each practice. The "customer service" staff (those that deal directly with the client) come from one of these three practices.

Project teams are then set up to deal with client projects as they come in. They will always include at least one member from Research and one from Design, with the remainder of the staff being a combination of people from each of the three disciplines, depending on the project.

Project managers are a part of the core team and are dedicated to that project, i.e., they have only one project on which they are working, and do not manage from afar – they are part of the day-to-day work of the team.

These teams also consist of members from the support staff; they are experts at particular pieces of project work. Teams also include specialists in business and communications. Additional support comes from SWAT teams – these teams come in for specialized situations, for example, the Analysis SWAT team, which may help to set up coding and data form structures. SWAT teams however, don't get handed to a team on a silver platter. Project managers need to make a case that one is needed and demonstrate its value on an ongoing basis.

What's different about E-Lab is that within each of these practices, besides responding to the demands of their workload, they are constantly asking themselves the question, "how can we do this better?" It's an important question for every team, every organization, but E-Lab has found it's the way to maintain a competitive edge.

Smart quotes

Everything comes to him who hustles while he waits.

Thomas Edison

In terms of their physical layout they have project rooms and very limited individual desk space. Each team has a home and is supported, in what may be simple ways, to keep the whole picture together by supporting the focus, materializing the data and supporting emerging models that teams may need.

I find nothing more silly than companies that say they have teams and the teams are so dispersed that they really work independently with the exception of a few co-ordination meetings. That is not what gets the most value out of interdisciplinary teams.

Rick Robinson (co-founder and principal at E-Lab)

SMART VOICES

Each team is provided with an "object of focus" which is understandable and makes sense to all of the disciplines, and it's more than just their goal. They create what is called a "hunt statement," which while similar to a project goal, differs in that the "object of focus" is a framework, built on everyone's underlying notion of experience. It emerges over the course of the project and it isn't defined at the beginning.

Core teams don't change, so the only people that may find themselves on more than one project at a time would be specialists. But even so, after a project is finished, team members find they are working with a whole new team. So how harmonious are things then? As you might expect, there are perfectly harmonious teams and teams that barely make it through the project. Only once have they had to reconstitute a team because of irreconcilable conflicts, but that's out of nearly 100 projects so far.

They've managed to keep teams together with the help of their conflict policy and a clearly ordered level of resolution identified. People know who to go to, who if that doesn't work, who if that doesn't work, and so on. And employees are evaluated on how well they honor commitments, complete the work, and respect team mates, and that means it matters to their salary. You've guessed right if you assume that people are working on this actively. The bonus is that it has created an environment where peer education can flourish.

Smart quotes

Amazing things happen when you make people feel they are valued as individuals, when you dignify their suggestions and their ideas, when you show your respect for them by allowing them to exercise their own wisdom and judgement and discretion.

Herb Kelleher (airline executive)

Teams set out "rules" or norms that everyone can work with, and it's usually done during the internal kickoff meeting. They also run an initiation meeting where the practice directors lay out key goals, likely problems and hurdles in the team, personnel and company area.

Now what?

Here are some ideas from E-Lab's style of working – is it possible to get them to work for you in your team/organization?

- Ask yourselves the question, "Can we do our job better?" If you are asking that question, what happens with the answers? Do you really act on the answers?

- Institute a conflict policy instead of turning a blind eye and hoping it will resolve itself – and that no one loses it in the process.

- Create practice communities – that means teams draw on the skills across the organization. Make it possible on a regular basis for people to contribute outside of their job description, role or department.

- Once your team has developed a goal, keep things open so that the "object of focus" can evolve, instead of freaking out because things aren't going "according to plan".

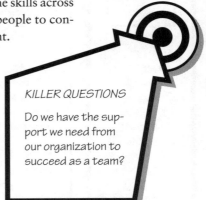

KILLER QUESTIONS

Do we have the support we need from our organization to succeed as a team?

- Change your evaluation system so that it hinges on how well you honor commitments, complete work and respect team mates.

E-Lab can be found at www.elab.com

The Bishopston Team

The Bishopston team of midwives is a collection of seven women who work as community midwives. They provide full coverage: pre-delivery and post-natal care. It also means that at least one midwife, with the back-up of another, needs to be on call 24 hours a day. While the concept of community midwifery is not uncommon, it doesn't exist everywhere. This particular team was one of the first to establish this system of care, and proved that it can be achieved.

They have a case load of over 30 pregnant women at any one time in their care, they run clinics preparing couples for the birthing experience, as well as being available for regular appointments, and emergencies. The logis-

SMART PEOPLE
TO HAVE ON
YOUR SIDE:

MICHAEL
MCNEAL,
DIRECTOR OF
CORPORATE
EMPLOYMENT,
CISCO
SYSTEMS, INC.

McNeal believes that great hiring requires creative marketing. "When it comes to staffing, we are the salesforce inside Cisco." They are the ones who "sell" Cisco every day. He analyzes his hiring channels in the same way that a marketing department would analyze its distribution channels. And their website is living proof of their creative marketing. At it, you can match skills with openings, submit a resumé online or create one using the site's resumé builder.

McNeal also hates Help Wanted Ads; he'd rather get more demographic than that. For example, they will have a stand at the Santa Clara Home and Garden Show assuming that homeowners in that area who can afford to own a home must be top achievers. They will also go to Stanford/Berkeley football games and spell out the website address during a Mexican wave.

He also believes you can hire well if you work in tandem with customers and suppliers, on the assumption that when more than one company sponsors an event you can create more interest.

He also has a software system in place that tracks his return on an "event" in terms of business cards, leads, interviews and new hires.

tics of coverage are tough, the hours are difficult and, to be a part of this team, or, as one midwife calls it, to "come out" (i.e. out of the hospital system), means you must be highly motivated. It also means that a midwife may not have a consistent relationship with all the clients, although they will each have a caseload for which they are ultimately responsible.

How do they make it work? They rely heavily on good communication systems, have a shared philosophy of the quality of care that should be provided, meet on a regular basis, and are very picky in their selection process when an opening occurs. There is always a team co-ordinator responsible for feeding-down information and drawing the team together, and this role rotates through the team.

While decision-making on cases will have to take place, usually on the spot, because they share the same philosophy of quality of care, they have a great deal of confidence in each other's competence and ability. They have developed a peer review to address what is good practice and run a clinical audit. They try to encourage each other to talk about issues that come up – and have a low tolerance for not discussing problems that may have arisen. Owning up to mistakes is encouraged, and while it may upset someone at the time, they have to rely on each other's honesty and openness to communicate a problem, otherwise they could be putting a couple of people's lives in danger.

Other decisions are made by the entire team, and not without discussion or debate. What they have learned is to take the time to discuss it. In the

- At what level are we comfortable sharing decision-making? Should it be increased?
- Do we share the same standard of quality with each other? Is it enough to develop a system where we really trust each other with our work?

KILLER QUESTIONS

past there was a problem when one midwife came up with an idea to share shifts with another community team, which would have taken a lot of pressure off each team. But because it was seen to be coming from one midwife and not a team decision, the whole idea was abandoned. It appeared that someone was trying to take over and gain more control on how things happened; while this was a perception rather than a reality, it was a great lesson for the team.

The benefits for the individuals who decide to come out are that they gain the whole picture on midwifery; if you stay in the hospital system you'd be more specialized, doing either delivery or pre- and post-care. As part of the team, not only have they gained knowledge, but usually get promoted very quickly.

Smart quotes

Teams depend on the ability of people to work interdependently in order to realize a common goal. Superior team performance is rarely found without high levels of trust.

Robert Bruce Shaw, *Trust in the Balance*

The two most important issues for this team are communication and the quality of their relationships with each other. They are operating with a very high level of trust, and in order to maintain that, they need to be very clear about what has happened on their shift. Without that, they could be compromising the next midwife, not to mention the patient.

Their communication system relies on recording each patient's history, email, and frequent in-depth conversations, especially during an on-call shift hand-over. The team meets in full twice a month, but ideally that could be more frequent. The meetings address any overall problems, issues or important information. They are important not only for sharing information, but they give the team a chance to be together. At these meetings they try to sort out problems, and this sometimes includes personality conflicts. While like any other team, they find that they may talk to others first before they address an individual they have a conflict with, they will all encourage each other to go and deal with that individual. One thing they have found that they can't afford is rifts within the team; they rely much too heavily on each other. Not to say this is done easily; even the individuals in the team who are outspoken and embrace the idea of dealing with conflict, find it very difficult. It's uncomfortable, but if it's not done, it can break down the trust too quickly in the team. Also they often have student midwifes working with them, with whom they must be honest.

One way in which they have developed trust is through their selection system. While the entire team is not involved in recruitment, they have found that they need to be very selective. Because the time demands of the job on an individual are so tough, they need to be very clear that someone coming in understands exactly what the job entails. Another issue is personality, and being sure that someone can fit in. Fitting-in has a great deal to do not only with how nice you are, but whether you can carry your load, develop the interpersonal skills needed to deal with patients and the rest of the team, own up to your actions and establish trust within the team very quickly.

> *Smart things to say about teams*
>
> Of course it's the same old story. Truth usually is the same old story.
>
> Margaret Thatcher (former British Prime Minister)

Now what?

Can you develop relationships that are based on high levels of trust in the same way that the Bishopston team have? Why not try by:

- setting-up a system where owning up to a mistake or problem is acceptable, that means not being penalized for making a mistake.

- setting-up a communication system between team members that's good enough so that you feel you can rely on everyone in the team.

- rotating team leadership within the team – that means developing good communication systems so that everyone understands what's important and what has to happen.

- getting everyone involved in all stages of work – that way you have the chance to gain experience, knowledge – and hopefully a better promotion, inside or outside the organization.

Outdoor Adventures

Instead of comparing the "rapidly changing business world" with whitewater rafting, let's look at a rafting company that's taken their lessons from the business world – Outdoor Adventures (OA). River rafting is seasonal work, it only happens when the water is running, and how much you'll get each season is, of course, dependent on the weather. This is a business that can earn money, even in a good year, for only 6 months, so they'd better be doing it right. OA runs 4 major rivers in the Western USA and even though water is their lifeline, they believe they have something just as valuable – their staff.

OA believes in teams, which is saying a lot. Because their "staff" changes year to year, you can't be guaranteed that your top or most experienced guides will be back next year – they may have to finish their university degree or get a job in the "real world." Add to this, the more opportunities a guide has to work on different rivers over their career, the more skilled they will be. So maintaining a team approach takes effort and understanding.

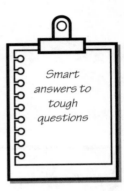

Q: We don't have time to get our work done, how can we find time to coach and advise team mates and colleagues?

A: Every organization's, every team's asset is its people, and the best way to hold on to them is to give them the opportunity to learn from each other. That learning is not only the organization's asset but the individual's. The more you have, the more valuable you become.

OA doesn't expect their staff to come together at each river – which can be hundreds of miles away – without any time to be together. At the beginning of each season a three-day meeting is run for all staff members, followed by three days on the water. And everyone is expected to be there. Besides being a time to find out what changes management has made and to brush up on skills, it's also a chance to see who's come back for another year, who's going to work on which river, as well as getting to know the new recruits. Most importantly it gives all the guides from each river the opportunity to meet as a team and spend some time thinking about what goals and approaches they are going to take given the available resources (water levels are key here) and skill levels of members.

Each river is staffed with a general manager and a core staff of guides who have requested which river they'd prefer to work on. The general manager tends to be a "retired" guide, who is expected to get on the water during the season to stay in touch.

For each trip there is a team of guides that work from the pool of guides available. Most trips run with a different combination of guides every time. In order to avoid anarchy on the water, there is always a designated Trip Leader (TL). The TL may or may not be the most experienced guide, and in fact it's often the least experienced. OA expects their more experienced guides to coach, advise and teach their least experienced guide. But whatever their experience, the TL's call is final.

River guides come from a wide spectrum of life, from the full-time guide who travels the world, to the big city lawyer taking a break from life as we know it. In order to keep this motley crew together, several things are important. First, everyone has a part to play, a safe-and-fun river trip means that guides respect each other – they don't necessarily like each other, but they have to respect their needs and are aware of each other's level of skill and confidence.

Second, there's a lot of grunt work that has to be done, from loading up rubber rafts and getting them down to the water, to cooking food for the guests, no one slacks off, not even the TL.

When you're on the water it's important that each guide is aware of every other boat on the water and that means looking out for each other. If you're lead boat flips, the second boat better be close enough to let the rest of the guides know so they can help pick up the pieces as they come downstream. The best trips for the customer and the guides are the ones where everyone knows what has to happen, whether there's carnage (as in flips or swimmers) or not.

After every trip there is a team debriefing, where guides get the opportunity to talk through and learn from the trip, whether it's a technique to use or a specific nasty spot on the water to look out for. It's also an opportunity to blow off some steam or just pop open a beer and toast a job well done.

OA's management team decided that they had to take teamwork a step further, that the only way they could provide outstanding customer service was to listen to their guides. So while they continue to promote teams, they also know that they must give their guides the power to change things.

As an author and consultant Block initiated the empowerment movement. He believes that in order to create organizations that "work," we need a shift not only in beliefs and attitudes, but in governance – how we distribute power, privilege, and the control of money.

Block believes that we've become compartmentalized in our lives. This is reflected in organizations, where people are task-oriented or people-oriented, hard-nosed or soft-nosed. With his idea of stewardship he believes we can reintegrate the parts of ourselves. And even though we may develop and successfully integrate a variety of programs to help keep our organizations happy and healthy – cost reduction, continuous improvement, customer service, and quality circles – he believes that the major part of our lives stays unchanged. "We remain watchful of people who have power over us; we feel that the organization is the creation of someone other than ourselves, and that the changes we want to make still need sponsorship or permission from others at a higher level."

He defines stewardship as the "umbrella idea which promises the means of achieving fundamental change in the way we govern our institutions." It is the choice to preside over the orderly distribution of power. This means giving people at the bottom and the boundaries of the organization choice over how to serve a customer, a citizen, or a community. Here you can see his belief in empowerment, but he takes stewardship a step further by saying that it is the willingness to be accountable for the well-being of the larger organization by operating in service, rather than in control, of those around us. It is accountability without control or compliance.

He is a proponent of teams but, as you would guess, empowered ones. "… efforts at implementing stewardship usually begin with some kind of team-building activity. Team-building is a good way of creating partnership in small groups; it can take the form of renegotiating the relationship between boss and subordinate, or creating open dialogue and clear expectations within a work group or across departmental boundaries. The intent though, is to do more than improve communication, it is to create a balance of power: accountability exchanged in both directions. Demands and requirements flowing both ways."

Block writes a monthly column that can be accessed at www.aqp.org/newssample.html

SMART PEOPLE TO HAVE ON YOUR SIDE:

PETER BLOCK

The manager at each river is expected to get ideas and suggestions from the guides on how to make the operation run more smoothly and, most importantly, implement some of them.

Now what?

Try developing the team and organization by:

- getting team members to respect each other, even if they don't like each other, by showing off individual's roles, levels of skills and competence, and how important everyone is to the success of the team

- making sure everyone does some grunt work, not just the new kid on the block; that means everyone feels a part and it breaks down the "hidden" or obvious hierarchy that exists

- making sure everyone on the team knows what is supposed to happen, great customer service comes when team members can anticipate each other's needs

- taking advice from the people who have direct contact with the client – and make changes based on that advice.

St. Luke's

St. Luke's advertising agency doesn't believe in corporate hierarchies. It's an agency that is owned by every one of its employees. St. Luke's was created with a co-operative structure called, Qualifying Employee Shareholder Trust (Quest). The vision of the founders was to form a company that is based on relationships rather than hierarchy, that is open, creative and employee-owned. The company is governed by Quest, which is a six-member council elected by the staff. This council is ultimately responsible for keeping in balance the three things that measure the company's health: finances, internal values and quality of output.

Aside from being stakeholders in the company, staff also set their own salaries and vacations and jointly "reinvent" the company's priorities every year. For example, last year they decided to set up a third division to make TV programs alongside their existing advertising and media departments.

St. Luke's structure has also demanded different working practices. Staff "hot desk" which means that no one has a permanent desk space and all physical resources are shared. Each new client is allocated a conference room, which is fitted out in the style and culture of the brand. So for example, the Eurostar brand room has actual seats from the train, and the Ikea room is furnished with furniture from the store. It's all about fostering creativity, and they believed to foster it they must break down bureaucracy.

There's also a billiard room, cafeteria and the Chillout Room, where staff can go to escape. Employees aren't treated as though they are in school or, in order to prove that they are working, they must be at their desks at 9 a.m. As long as they create great work, they can do it in their own time.

But reconfiguring the office space is not what it's all about: many companies have tried to change the workplace to redefine the atmosphere, but

Smart quotes

All power is trust.

Benjamin Disraeli (former British Prime Minister)

We believe that good work comes from a balance of listening and challenging.

St. Luke's advertising agency

SMART VOICES

the focus has become the office, and not the philosophy behind the reconfiguration.

St. Luke's is criticized by many in the advertising world. Many see it as too utopian and that it has a holier-than-thou attitude. But they believe that their campaigns work well because the whole of the company wants to work with the client.

St. Luke's claims to be the world's first ethical, stakeholding advertising agency, and that the truth about the advertiser will be the only communication that matters in the future. So for example, when Monsanto (the biotechnology company) came to them, St. Luke's staff held a meeting. They felt uncomfortable about pitching for the work, and decided to angle their pitch to Monsanto so that the advertising would expose both sides of the biotechnology debate. (Monsanto didn't take things further.) They feel they've developed their own philosophy of work and hope to be able to devise ways of communicating it.

St. Luke's also doesn't enter award competitions, which single-out one person and not the team that has done the work.

St. Luke's is not trying to be a "nicey-nicey" advertising agency. They believe that good advertising is sometimes provocative and that all organizations should conduct themselves ethically. They admit, however, that ultimately they are trying to sell more stuff.

Smart things to say about teams

Adversarial power relationships work only if you never have to see or work with the bastards again.

Peter Drucker (management thinker and author)

Now what?

Why don't you try the following?

- Run an ethical meeting with staff to decide if everyone is willing to work with a "controversial" client.

- Create a client environment by bringing the client into your office – either by getting them to come and work side-by-side or creating their environment within yours.

- Trust everyone will create great work and ban fixed office hours.

TEAMWORK AT VIRGIN COMPANIES

Building businesses is much better than buying them, which in the eighties was sadly forgotten. Within the Virgin group, all our companies are home-grown by teams of competent people. We give them the necessary resources and leave them to get on with it.

Industry is at its exciting best in companies run by small, enthusiastic teams, built from scratch, with everything to prove. These circumstances attract the brightest people and bring out the highest levels of effort, creativity and flexibility. They also encourage responsiveness to customer needs and the willingness to react to fast-changing circumstances as a challenge. There could be no greater contrast to some large, declining companies which struggle to survive by ignoring changing circumstances in the hope that they will go away.

Sources include *Director Annual Convention Special* (Institute of Directors, April 1994); "Management maketh man – how the hell does Branson manage it?", *Management Weekly*, July 1991.

SMART VOICES

- Get employees to measure the company's health by measuring finances, internal values and quality of output.

- In award competitions, enter only teams and not individuals.

St. Luke's can be reached at www.stlukes.co.uk.

You've had a chance to look at some interesting organizations that have created environments which they believe run closely to their ethics. Are they better because of it? Are they more successful because of the way they organize themselves? I guess it comes down to the question of how you measure success.

Index

how to make it work 180–83
information
    intuitive 177
    sensing 177
orientation
    judgement 177
    perception 177
preference for 183
teams 184–5
    job determination 186
    progress checks 186
    right representation 185–6
    right types 186
Myers, Isabel Briggs 175
    profile 178

Napoleon Bonaparte, quotes 103, 187
Nelson, Bob 165
neurolinguistic programming (NLP)
    chunking up, down, sideways 55–6
    defined 54
    delete, distort, generalize 54–5
    described 53–6, 70
Nolle, Tom, quote 62

Orwell, George, quote 141
Outdoor Adventures (OA) 210–12, 214

Parker, Glenn 108
    quote 44
Peters, Tom 23
Phillips, Donald 57
Phillips, Nicola 50, 83
problems 107–9
    conflict 125–7, 129–31
    defensiveness
        agreeing too quickly 135
        blaming others/circumstances
            beyond your control 135
        changing the subject 136

        denial/rejection of information
            135
        lying 135
    disruptive behavior 131–2
        alienation from team 132
        confronting 140–41
        dealing with 136–41
        disagreement with goals 132
        diverting 139
        externalizing 139–40
        feeling that goals are out of line
            with organization's 133
        intellectualizing 137–8
        lack of interest in task/goals 133
        misunderstanding goals 133
        not being able to get own way 133
        not being able to get point across
            133
        not understanding what is being
            said 133
        not understanding why you are
            there 133
    geography 113–14
    I am not a team player 116–18
    leadership 118
        disruptive 119
        doesn't buy into teamwork 118
        leads in different direction from
            company strategy 119
        leads from too far in front 119
        no vision/direction 118
        non-specific goals 118
        solutions 120
    levels of communication 123
        facts/information 123
        feelings/emotions 124
        ideas/judgements 123
        ritual/cliché 123
        values 124
    meetings 115